WILLIAMS-SONOMA

MASTERING

Grilling & Barbecuing

Author
RICK RODGERS

General Editor
CHUCK WILLIAMS

Photographers
TUCKER & HOSSLER

NEW YORK · LONDON · TORONTO · SYDNEY

Contents

About this book

While the idea of firing up the grill to cook dinner appeals to nearly everyone, it can also be intimidating. But once you have cooked your way through *Mastering Grilling & Barbecuing* and learned the fundamentals of successful grilling, you will have the confidence to prepare dozens of time-honored dishes, including herb-rubbed T-bone steaks, salmon cooked on a cedar plank, spicy pork satay, and brined whole chicken. You will also learn the secrets of true, slow-smoked dishes from the top three barbecue regions of the world—beef brisket from Texas, pork shoulder from North Carolina, and ribs from Kansas City.

Here is how this book acts as a master class in grilling and barbecuing: In the opening pages, you will learn about the three primary grilling methods—direct heat, indirect heat, and smoking—and their respective attributes. You will also discover which foods are best for grilling and how to judge when they are done; how to flavor foods with spice rubs, marinades, brines, and wood chips; how to control your fire's heat; how to handle both your food and your grill safely; and how to garnish and serve grilled foods. This introductory information is followed by the Basic Recipes chapter, which contains a quartet of indispensable recipes for traditional grilling, including a spice rub, two barbecue sauces, and a versatile rich chicken stock. Next, the Key Techniques chapter demonstrates important cooking skills that will be applied throughout the book, such as how to build a fire in a charcoal grill, how to use wood chips for barbecuing, and how to create professional-looking grill marks on your foods. Finally, the recipes are divided into three chapters by grilling method or by type of food.

With this comprehensive book by your side, you are ready to fire up your grill and get started on becoming a master of backyard grilling.

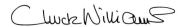

Working with the Recipes

While culinary success always depends on the details, this is especially true for grilling and barbecuing, methods that call for building and maintaining a fire. But before you are ready to light the charcoal or depress the gas grill igniter, you need to develop the skills that will have you grilling with confidence. In the following pages, you will learn those key skills, which you will then put to work making reliable recipes fit for any occasion.

This book is organized so that you learn the key skills first, then build on them. Each chapter is anchored by at least one master recipe, which teaches you how to make a classic dish step-by-step, with both words and pictures.

After you complete the master recipes, the other recipes in the chapters will help you to continue your learning. As you make these shorter recipes, many of which include photographs illustrating any difficult techniques, your confidence will grow. Some recipes also include

variations, which will dramatically increase your grilling repertory.

With this book, you'll learn how to become an expert in all aspects of grilling. You'll know when to use direct or indirect heat, the characteristics of both gas and charcoal grills, and how to infuse food with smoke. For example, the recipe for Classic Hamburgers on page 47 explains exactly what kind of beef to use for the best results; how to chop the meat at home; the proper way to form patties; cooking instructions for both gas and charcoal

grills; and how to test for doneness. And once you've mastered this classic version, there are six tempting burger variations with which you can put your newfound knowledge to work.

The secret behind success is practice. As you learn each new master recipe, you will become more comfortable and efficient at the grill. Remember that any time you spend at the grill hones your skills. To find out more about the key tools and equipment you will need for grilling, turn to pages 132–33.

Grill Types & Grilling Methods

Traditionally, grilling has meant cooking food directly over a charcoal fire. While this is the best-known method, it isn't the only way to grill. Grilling is full of equipment and fuel options, from charcoal to propane to natural gas. It is also full of cooking options, which means that the best way to grill salmon fillets is not the best way to grill a beef brisket. Grilling experts carefully pair foods with their ideal cooking method: direct heat, indirect heat, or smoking.

Grill Types

Grills are most commonly fueled by charcoal or gas. While a gas grill cannot match the flavor of charcoal-cooked food, a charcoal grill cannot match the simple operation and easy cleanup of a gas grill. I own one of each, using the gas grill when quick-and-easy preparation is the goal, and the charcoal grill for weekend meals when I have more time.

Most charcoal grills are kettle shaped, although there are square or rectangular braziers and even egg-shaped models. Vents on the base and cover alter oxygen flow, controlling the interior temperature for indirect-heat grilling and smoking. The charcoal is arranged on a grate, or fire bed, in the bottom of the kettle, and the grill grate for holding the food sits above it. While there are larger and smaller models, I used the standard 22½-inch (57-cm) diameter grill to develop the recipes in this book. Admittedly, charcoal is bulky and difficult to transport, and its ashes can be a disposal headache. But the inarguable virtue of a charcoal grill is its heat, which creates the desired browned exterior and a smoky flavor. These are the touchstones of perfectly grilled food.

The easy operation of gas grills has made them extremely popular. The smaller models, fueled by tanks of liquid propane, can be moved around outside, while larger ones are often hooked up permanently to a natural-gas line. Yesteryear's lava rocks have mostly disappeared, replaced by metal bars or other diffusing materials heated by a propane flame, which evenly distributes heat throughout the cooking area. While food cooked on a gas grill lacks distinctive charcoal flavor, you can use wood chips to infuse the food with aromatic smoke. If you are interested in convenience and you have a reliable supply of fuel, it is hard to disparage the gas grill's convenience.

Regardless of the grill you choose, there are three distinct methods you will use: direct heat, indirect heat, and smoking.

Methods of Grilling

If you cook food directly over the heat source, be it charcoal or gas, you are cooking by direct heat. The heat is high and intense, and best for relatively thin food that will cook within 20 minutes (burgers, meat and fish steaks, chops, and skewered food). Flare-ups—when the fat drips and causes flames to grow—are a negative side effect of direct-heat grilling, but there are ways to tame them (see Controlling the Heat, page 14).

Indirect heat is recommended for large pieces of food, such as roasts, whole chickens, and beef and pork ribs, that would burn before they are done if cooked over direct heat. With this grilling method, one or two areas of the grill are heated, and the food is placed in the unheated area. The grill is covered, and moderate heat radiates around the food much in the same way that food cooks in an oven. Usually, a disposable aluminum pan with liquid is placed in the unheated area of the grill to catch the dripping fat and juices from the food. The steam from the liquid helps moisten the food as it cooks.

Smoking is a type of indirect grilling in which the food is cooked by low to moderate heat with the addition of wood chips, which imparts a smoky flavor. Barbecuing is similar, although it is usually reserved for large cuts that need long, slow cooking to melt away fat and connective tissues. When barbecuing, the wood chips must be added in several additions during the long cooking time. The barbecue classics, beef brisket and pork shoulder, are great examples of the technique.

Covering the Grill

There is wide debate about whether or not to cover the grill when grilling over direct heat. Critics say that covering the grill makes it more like roasting than grilling. Others claim that covering a charcoal grill may effect the flavor of the food. I find that covering the grill helps food cook more evenly and prevents flare-ups. I always cover the grill when direct-heat grilling, even though I will have to clean the inside of the cover more often (see page 15).

Food for the Grill

Some foods simply taste better cooked on a grill. Of course, you can fry a steak on the stove top, but that same steak grilled over hot coals is exceptional. Every second it spends on the grill goes toward delivering a deliciously browned crust and a smoky flavor that appeals to nearly everyone. But not every food is a candidate for grilling, and the method—direct heat, indirect heat, smoking—you use will vary depending on what you are cooking.

Meats

Beef, pork, lamb, and veal all illustrate how grilling can enhance the flavors of foods. Every cut, from a roast to a steak, gets a crisp, burnished brown exterior and a wonderful smoky taste.

The fat content of the cut will help to determine how you grill the meat and its final flavor and juiciness. The intramuscular fat in well-marbled meat bastes from the inside out, so you will need only minimal enhancement, such as in Grilled T-Bone Steaks with Thyme-

Garlic Paste (page 54). Lean cuts, such as flank steak or skirt steak, will benefit from a moisture-boosting marinade. Carne Asada and its variations (pages 59–61) is a good example. Fat content also plays a role in the selection of ground (minced) meat for the grill. If it is too lean, your burgers will most likely be dry and flavorless. In general, thin steaks and burgers are cooked over direct heat, while thicker or fattier cuts, like beef brisket or pork shoulder, are grilled over indirect heat or by smoking.

Poultry

Birds, such as chicken, turkey, and duck, can be cooked whole or cut into parts. Grilling poultry with the skin on protects it against drying out, though you will need to cook it over indirect heat to avoid fat from the skin melting into the fire and causing flare-ups.

Seafood

Fish and shellfish can be successfully grilled if care is taken to choose the right candidates. Sturdy fish fillets and steaks,

such as salmon, swordfish, mahimahi, halibut, tuna, striped bass, and snapper, all work well on the grill, as do fish skewers. Grilled whole fish are wonderful, and are easy to turn if enclosed in a hinged wire basket. Shrimp (prawns) need only be cleaned and skewered. Mussels, clams, and oysters can be put into a frying pan to catch their juices and grilled over indirect heat.

Avoid thin, delicate fish fillets like flounder and sole, as they tend to fall apart when turned on the grill. Also, lightly oil any fish and make sure the grate is clean before you begin grilling, and use moderately hot direct heat to avoid overcooking.

Fresh Produce

Vegetables and fruits are prime choices for grilling, usually over direct heat. Use the freshest, in-season produce you can find, as flaws tend to be amplified, not hidden, by the grill. Tender vegetables cooked over direct heat, such as eggplants (aubergines), summer squashes, and tomatoes, make great side dishes, salsas, and main courses. Firmer vegetables call for additional steps: Potatoes are partially cooked in boiling water to shorten their grilling time, and sliced onions are softened in aluminum foil packets to trap the steam given off by their juices. Grilled in its husks to prevent scorching, corn on the cob is a summertime dinner-table icon.

Grilled firm-fleshed fruits such as peaches, plums, nectarines, pineapple, and mangoes make terrific desserts. Be especially sure to scrub the grate clean of any residual sauces or drippings before you start.

The Grilling Pantry

Your pantry probably already holds many ingredients used in grilling. For example, dried spices and herbs, such as cumin, fennel seeds, oregano, thyme, paprika, red pepper flakes, and onion and garlic powders, are typically used in spice rubs and sauces. Tomato ketchup, hot-pepper sauce, vinegar, mustard, and Worcestershire sauce play important roles in basting and table sauces. Asian staples like soy sauce, fish sauce, and hoisin sauce turn up in marinades and dipping sauces. Finally, nuts add flavor to salsas, compound butters, and stuffings.

Flavoring Grilled Foods

Your grill's heat source, be it charcoal or gas, provides distinctive grilling characteristics that translate into flavor. But there are several ways to give grilled foods even more flavor. They can be rubbed with spice blends or pastes, marinated or brined in aromatic liquids, infused with smoke from wood chips, basted with barbecue sauces, or topped with an herb-flecked compound butter—all with excellent results.

There are three opportunities to add flavor to grilled food: before, during, and after the grilling process. Some recipes take advantage of all three.

Before grilling is the most common time to season foods. Marinating adds flavor and moisture, as illustrated in Carne Asada and its variations (pages 59–61), while Herb-Brined Whole Chicken (page 105) shows how brining is a particularly efficient way to add moisture. Surface seasonings, such as herb and spice rubs and pastes, can be made and applied quickly, as in Shrimp Skewers with Barbecue Spices (page 83).

Natural flavor-packed smoke is created by fat and juices dripping onto hot coals or the heating elements of a gas grill in Classic Hamburgers (page 47) or by soaked wood chips in Maple-Smoked Salmon Steaks (page 114). As they cook in the aromatic smoke, barbecued meats, such as Texas Beef Brisket (page 87), are often slathered with a "mopping" sauce to keep their surfaces moist and to infuse them with flavor. And Classic Grilled Chicken with Barbecue Sauce (page 110) shows what a first-rate barbecue sauce can do for grilled chicken.

The fuel you use for your grill also enhances or inhibits the flavor of your food. For years, the only way to fire up a grill was with charcoal briquettes. Briquettes burn evenly and can be found at any market. Pure hardwood charcoal (mesquite, hickory, alder, oak, maple, and birch) is increasingly available, and some cooks prefer its natural flavor. It burns hotter and more quickly than briquettes and is therefore ideal for foods quickly cooked over direct heat, such as steaks and burgers. But hardwood charcoal comes in a variety of shard sizes, and the small chunks can burn to ashes in no time, while the big ones take longer. I like to mix equal amounts of charcoal briquettes and hardwood charcoal to combine their best features.

Finally, you can add flavor after grilling. Some dishes, such as Pork Satay with Peanut Sauce and variations (pages 62–65), are paired with distinct sauces for dipping.

Steaks (both meat and fish), chops, and vegetables are often topped with a savory relish or salsa for lots of added flavor. Barbecue sauce can be passed at the table for guests to slather on chicken or ribs, while a pat of a compound butter will enhance fish or an ear of fresh corn, as well as grilled stone fruits.

Keep It Natural

Lighter fluid and "easy-light" (self-igniting) briquettes are convenient, but the overpowering chemical flavor is easily transferred to your food. Also, many authorities believe these products are harmful to the environment. I prefer to use a chimney starter (see page 38) to start a fire in a charcoal grill. Its benefits are many: it is inexpensive, safe, and easy to use, and it will not impart undesirable flavors to your foods.

Evaluating Doneness

Because of the variables inherent in cooking outdoors on an outdoor grill, it is common for novice grillers to end up with overdone steak or raw poultry. Armed with the information in this section, you'll become knowledgeable on how to judge when your food is perfectly cooked. There are four ways to determine doneness—temperature, texture, sight, and touch. Here, you will learn the best test to use for a variety of grilled foods.

Temperature Test

Using an instant-read or digital probe thermometer is the most reliable way to test meat and poultry. Always insert the thermometer away from bone, which can skew the reading. The United States Department of Agriculture (USDA) has specific minimum temperature standards for many foods. Many cooks ignore these recommendations, and assume the small risk. But, if you prefer absolute safety over taste, be sure to follow the guidelines available on the USDA website.

Texture Test

A texture test is used for items too thin or delicate to test with a thermometer. For example, inserting the tip of a knife or the tines of a fork into a fish fillet reveals if the flesh flakes and is therefore done. You can also test grilled vegetables and fruits this way.

Sight Test

A sight test is often quick and easy. Shellfish, for example, will turn from translucent to opaque, while cooked poultry will reveal clear juices when the flesh is pierced with a knife. You can check the color of a steak or chop by making a small slit into the flesh. But do this sparingly, as it can cause the loss of flavorful juices.

Touch Test

This final test is ideal for steaks and chops. Press against the meat with your fingertips: rare meat will be relatively soft, medium somewhat firm, and well-done will be quite firm.

Controlling the Heat

Taming the fire of a charcoal grill can be a challenge. Is the fire so hot that the food is burning? Is the fire so cool that the food is barely cooking? Juices and fat from the food can drip onto coals and heating elements, causing flare-ups. To sidestep these problems, you need to understand the characteristics of the different kinds of fuel and to know how to create separate heat zones in the grill to modulate the heat.

Many people prepare a fire in a charcoal grill by spreading the hot coals in a thick, even layer, or in a gas grill by turning all of the heat elements to high. Both techniques guarantee flare-ups and burned food.

Instead, you need to divide the cooking area into separate heating zones. By creating both hot and cooler areas, you can control the cooking speed. For example, you can sear food over the hottest section, and then move it to the cooler area to complete cooking. Heating zones ensure safer cooking, too. When fat drips onto the heat source and causes flames to flare up, you can move food to the cooler section. For more information on setting up heat zones, see page 38.

The type of fuel is a factor, too. Propane and gas are steady, reliable heat sources, but they do not burn as hot as a charcoal fire. Because briquettes are uniform, they give off steady heat, but they eventually burn down and must be replenished after about 30 minutes. The safest way to add more briquettes is to carefully lift off the grill grate and quickly add more as needed. Some experienced grillers will add the briquettes through a slot in the grate as well. Hardwood charcoal burns the hottest of all, but it will also burn more quickly. See the chart on page 16 for how to test for grill temperatures.

The vents on a charcoal grill are also used to control heat, as fire needs oxygen to burn—open for a hotter fire and closed, but not completely, for a slower fire—while an easy dial does the same on a gas grill.

Grilling Safety

From lighting the fire to extinguishing it, cooks must follow the safety rules that specifically pertain to grilling. Never forget that you are working with an open flame and that even the outside surface of the grill has the potential to burn an unwary person or pet. Most of the rules are simply common sense, however, and will become second nature after you have fired up your grill just a few times.

Grill Safety

Grill safety begins with the cook's clothing. Avoid loose clothing and tie back long hair. Do not grill barefoot and avoid sandals or flip-flops. Closed shoes are much better protection against stray coals and sparks. Protect your hands with long, thick oven mitts, and use long-handled grilling tools. (See pages 132–33 for recommended tools.)

Choose the location of your grill carefully. Grills are intended for outside use only and should never be used in an enclosed area. Carbon monoxide is deadly and invisible. Place the grill away from any tree branches or overhanging building elements, such as eaves or awnings. If you must grill on a wood deck, hose it down well to discourage sparks from igniting. Have a garden hose or fire extinguisher handy, in case of a threatening fire.

When building your fire, follow these important rules. In a charcoal grill, never use lighter fluid, kerosene, or gas. They are highly combustible and thus extremely dangerous. Ignite the charcoal by using a chimney starter. (See page 38 for instructions on how to use a chimney starter.) Pour the ignited coals from the chimney starter, holding the handle with a thick oven mitt, and find a safe, fireproof place to put the hot chimney.

In a gas grill, always ignite the heat elements with the cover open to keep gas from collecting under the lid. If the elements fail to ignite, turn the elements and the tank valve off for at least 5 minutes before trying again.

After grilling on a charcoal grill, cover the grill and close the vents. Let the ash cool for at least 24 hours before discarding. On a gas grill, turn off the burners and the fuel source.

Cleaning the Interior of the Grill

Many people are worried about the flaky black material coating the inside of their charcoal grill cover. That's carbon buildup and should be scraped off with a wire brush if it's visible. The entire grill interior should be cleaned with a commercial grill cleaner twice a year, usually at the beginning and end of the traditional grilling season. Be sure to hose down the grill to remove residual cleaner before cooking on it. Gas grill owners should follow the manual for cleaning gas jets, which may mean dismantling the grill. While the grill is apart, scrub the interior with hot soapy water to remove grease buildup and rinse well.

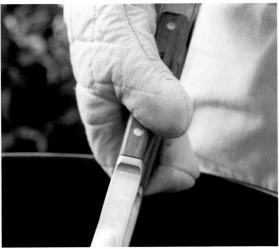

Food Safety

Grilling goes hand in hand with warm summer weather. Unfortunately, so do food-borne illnesses. While risk is intensified during the hotter months of the year, it is actually present year-round. To guard against such problems, be sure to stay within the recipe guidelines of keeping meat at room temperature. Another important and easy-to-follow guideline is always to check the sell-by and use-by dates on any food before you purchase it.

Food safety is an important concern throughout the year, but even more so during the summer grilling season, as bacteria grow readily in a warm environment. But to ensure that foods cook evenly on the grill, they should not be ice cold, so most of the recipes in this book suggest removing the foods from the refrigerator an hour before grilling. Although some sources will recommend removing them earlier, I have found that this "chill-off" period is both safe and sufficient. Also, never thaw frozen food at room temperature; instead, thaw it in the refrigerator or in a microwave oven.

Wash your hands well with hot, soapy water before and after handling raw meat, poultry, fish, or shellfish. In grilling, there are many opportunities for these raw ingredients to come into contact with basting sauces, marinades, and other foods, which can raise the risk of cross contamination. Sauces and marinades cause a particular food-safety problem, as they are sometimes served with the finished food. If you are basting with a marinade that held raw food, boil the marinade for 2 minutes and then let cool before using, or stop using the basting liquid 5 minutes before finishing cooking. Never serve a basting sauce that has been in contact with raw food. The basting brush can carry bacteria between the sauce and the food. A safer option is to prepare a double batch of sauce, or if you make only one batch, set aside some for serving before you use the balance. Also, never return cooked foods to the same platters or plates you used to carry the raw foods outside without washing them first.

Foods that are undercooked pose a safety threat, too. Purchase a high-quality instant-read thermometer or digital probe thermometer to measure internal temperatures, and follow the chart on page 17 to be sure that your food is cooked to the proper temperature.

Finally, let all hot items cool completely before storing them. A hot sauce in the refrigerator could cause the temperature inside to rise to a level that encourages bacteria to grow. You should also try to keep separate cutting boards for meat, poultry, and produce to avoid the risk of cross contamination.

The True Meaning of Barbecue

In the modern vernacular, the word *barbecued* is often used interchangeably with the word *grilled*. However, purists would never call the classic backyard cookout dish of chicken coated with the tangy tomato-based sauce "barbecued" chicken.

True barbecue calls for cooking food over a slow indirect-heat hardwood fire with lots of smoke. Think Texas Beef Brisket (page 87), North Carolina Pulled Pork (page 93), and Barbecued Beef Ribs (page 98).

GRILL TEMPERATURES

HEAT OF THE GRILL

Please note that heat may vary on different grills. This test is for a charcoal grill, as gas grills will come with a built-in temperature gauge. For the hand test, hold your hand, palm down, 4 inches (10 cm) above the fire.

HEAT LEVEL	TEMPERATURE	HAND TEST
Very high	450°F (230°C) and higher	Less than 1 second
High	400°–450°F (200°–230°C)	1 or 2 seconds
Medium-high	375°–400°F (190°–200°C)	2 or 3 seconds
Medium	350°–375°F (180°–190°C)	3 or 4 seconds
Medium-low	325°–350°F (165°–180°C)	4 or 5 seconds
Low	300°–325°F (150°–165°C)	5 seconds or more

Temperatures are taken before the resting period; they will rise 5°–10°F (3°–6°C) during this time.	ITEM	RARE	MEDIUM-RARE	MEDIUM	MEDIUM-WELL	WELL
	Beef	130°F (54°C)	140°F (60°C)	145°F (63°C)	150°F (65°C)	160°F (71°C) or more
	Chicken					170°F (76°C)
	Pork			145°–150°F (62°–65°C)	150°–160°F (65°C–71°C)	160°F (71°C) or more
	Duck					175°F (79°C)

The Resting Period

Many foods you remove from the grill—roasts, whole birds, and thick steaks—should be allowed to sit, undisturbed, at room temperature for a period of time before you carve, slice, or serve them. During cooking, heat forces the juices to the center of the meat or poultry, drying the edges in the process. If the food is carved without first resting, the exterior will be dry and the juices will flow out of the center onto the cutting board. But if it is allowed to rest before it is served, the juices will redistribute themselves throughout the food, ensuring that it is uniformly juicy.

The resting period ranges from 5 to 20 minutes, depending on the size of the food. The food retains heat when it is removed from the grill, and while it rests its internal temperature can rise 5°–10°F (3°–6°C). This is known as *carryover cooking*, and the larger the food and the longer it spent on the grill, the more its temperature will rise. Keep this in mind, with meats that you prefer rare or medium-rare. Once meat is overcooked, it can't be reversed.

The chart above shows the ideal temperatures for meats and poultry for a variety of doneness levels. Because of carryover cooking, these foods will reach their optimum temperature while resting.

Preparing Ingredients for Grilling

Grilling, like every kind of cooking, goes more smoothly when you are well organized. This means not only knowing how to set up the grill but also having all your ingredients prepared and measured and close at hand, so that you never need to stop to mix a sauce or chop an onion once you start cooking. Being organized is especially important when you are trying a recipe for the first time and you need to focus your full attention on the fire.

The best way to feel confident about grilling is to roll up your sleeves and try it. There is no good substitute for old-fashioned experience.

First, learn how to build an efficient charcoal fire (see page 9) or how to ignite your gas grill. Then, no matter what type of grill you have, master the concept of heat zones (see page 14). Finally, apply the tenets of both grilling and food safety (see pages 15–17), and you are on your way to becoming a master griller.

Having your ingredients organized is important, too. *Mise en place* is a culinary concept that every good cook needs to adopt. French for "put in place," this saying originated in professional kitchens and called for trimming, chopping, or otherwise preparing the food for the day's menus so that it was ready when an order was placed. The practice lives on in today's restaurant kitchens.

The home cook can easily do the same thing. First, read through a recipe carefully, paying close attention to how and when the ingredients are prepared. Then prepare and measure the ingredients as directed and put them in small bowls or ramekins, so they are ready to go.

Opaque cups are used for measuring dry ingredients, such as flour or sugar, and clear cups are used for liquids. A level measurement applies to both. (This is true for American cooks, who mainly cook by volume measures, while cooks elsewhere usually weigh dry ingredients.) Dry measuring cups come in standard sets of ⅛, ¼, ⅓, ½, and 1 cup. For a level measurement, heap the dry ingredient in the cup with a scoop or spoon and then sweep off the excess with the back of a knife, so the ingredient is level with the rim of the cup. Use the same cups for measuring leafy herbs, such as basil or parsley, packing them firmly, and sticky or semisolid ingredients, such as peanut butter or mayonnaise.

Liquid measuring cups are made of transparent tempered glass or plastic, so that you can see the ingredient inside, and have a pour spout. A well-stocked kitchen has 1-cup (8–fl oz/250-ml), 2-cup (16–fl oz/500-ml), and 4-cup (32–fl oz/1-l) liquid measures. To measure a liquid, pour it into the measuring cup to the appropriate mark on the side, put the cup on the countertop, let the liquid settle, and then check it at eye level to be accurate.

Measuring spoons, which come in standard increments of ⅛, ¼, ½, and 1 teaspoon, and 1 tablespoon, are found most often in nesting sets and are used for small, level amounts of both dry ingredients, such as herbs or spices, and liquids, such as soy sauce.

Garnishing & Serving Grilled Foods

Gone are the days when grilling was limited to such backyard favorites as barbecued chicken and hamburgers. Now, with restaurants serving more internationally inspired menus and everyone more interested in the dishes of different cultures, foods grilled at home look as good as they taste. A sprinkle of fresh herbs, a dusting of an aromatic and colorful spice blend, and an artful drizzle of sauce are just three ways to add flair to your grilled dishes.

Grilled foods, such as chicken or burgers, are traditionally served informally, either piled on platters or on a buffet table. But nowadays, grilling is becoming the way to cook for company as well. For example, Tea-Smoked Duck with Lemongrass Paste (page 113), served with a dipping sauce and showered with cilantro (fresh coriander), is not the typical paper-napkin backyard grill fare.

You can also easily add style to even your most casual meals. You might sprinkle chopped fresh herbs, chosen to complement the flavors of the recipe, over a finished dish for a nice green contrast. Small whole herb sprigs can be used, too, for individual servings, like grilled chicken breasts. Sauces make delicious and visually interesting accents, such as those drizzled on sliced flank steak in Carne Asada and its variations (pages 59–61). White plates show off nearly any food well. Or, pick a color that complements the warm brown hue of grilled recipes. Red, orange, and yellow are all good choices.

Beloved side dishes for grilled foods—slaws, potato and pasta salads, and simply prepared vegetables—are well known, but there's no reason for them to be ordinary. Offer napa cabbage slaw or a ginger-scented rice salad with Asian grilled dishes. Experiment with classic potato salad by using unusual vinegars or herb-flavored mustards. And rather than using a simple pat of butter, slather an herb-flecked compound butter on corn on the cob or an almond-infused butter to top off grilled fruit.

1

Basic Recipes

In this chapter, you will find an all-purpose spice rub that can be used to flavor poultry, pork, or fish headed for the grill, and you will learn how to make a rich chicken stock for use in dipping sauces to serve with your grilled foods. And no grilling book would be complete without a first-rate barbecue sauce. I offer two: a traditional tomato-based sauce and an intriguing mustard-rosemary sauce.

Basic Spice Rub

An all-purpose spice blend is one of the secrets to successful outdoor cooking. Rubbed onto chicken, pork, or salmon before grilling, this mixture provides lots of flavor for just a few seconds of effort. I like to toast my spices before grinding them; it really enhances the flavor of the rub.

2 teaspoons cumin seeds

1 teaspoon fennel seeds

2 tablespoons Spanish smoked paprika or sweet Hungarian paprika

2 teaspoons dried thyme

2 teaspoons dried sage

2 teaspoons dried oregano

2 teaspoons salt

2 teaspoons freshly ground black pepper

1½ teaspoons garlic powder

1½ teaspoons onion powder

1 teaspoon cayenne pepper

MAKES ABOUT ½ CUP (1½ OZ/45 G), ENOUGH FOR ABOUT 6 LB (3 KG) MEAT OR POULTRY

1 Toast the cumin and fennel

Toasting whole spices before grinding heats up their essential oils and makes them more pungent. Heat a small, dry frying pan over medium heat. (This jumpstarts the toasting process so that the seeds begin to toast as soon as they hit the hot surface of the pan.) Hold your hand, palm down, over the pan. If you can feel the heat rising, dip your fingers into cold water and then flick the water onto the pan. If, when the droplets hit the pan, they dance briefly over the hot surface and then evaporate almost immediately, the pan is ready for the seeds. Add the cumin and fennel seeds and toast, stirring or shaking the pan constantly, until the seeds are very fragrant and are toasted a slightly deeper shade of brown, about 1 minute; you may see a wisp or two of smoke rising from the pan. Remove from the heat. For more information on toasting seeds, turn to page 36.

2 Let the seeds cool

Immediately transfer the toasted seeds to a mortar or an electric spice grinder and let cool completely, about 10 minutes. Cooling the seeds allows them to crisp and makes grinding more efficient.

3 Grind the seeds

If you are working with a mortar, use a pestle to crush the cooled seeds, pressing it firmly against the seeds and rotating it against the sides of the mortar. Continue to grind until all the seeds are coarsely ground in small pieces measuring about ¹⁄₁₆ inch (2 mm). You want them to have some texture, not be ground to a powder. If using an electric coffee mill or spice grinder, pulse the machine on and off continually until the cooled seeds are coarsely ground, about ¹⁄₁₆ inch pieces.

4 **Mix the rub ingredients**
Transfer the ground cumin and fennel to a small airtight container with a secure lid. Add the paprika, thyme, sage, oregano, salt, black pepper, garlic powder, onion powder, and cayenne. Using the handle of the wooden spoon as your tool, stir and mix well to combine the spices and herbs thoroughly. Paprika has a tendency to clump up, so be sure to press firmly so that you break up the clumps and incorporate the spice evenly into the mixture.

5 **Store the spice rub**
Cover the container tightly with the lid. Store in a cool, dark place for up to 3 months. Dried herbs and spices lose their flavor over time, so it is best to make the rub in small batches that will be used within a 3-month period. Before each use, mix ingredients again to ensure that the flavors are evenly distributed.

CHEF'S TIP
If you don't have either a mortar and pestle or a spice grinder, you can crush the toasted cumin and fennel with a heavy pan. Place the cooled seeds on a work surface and use the bottom of a small, clean, heavy frying pan or saucepan to crush them coarsely.

Brown Poultry Stock

This is my favorite all-purpose stock to have on hand in the freezer. It has a rich but neutral chicken flavor, which is perfect for supplementing dipping sauces to pair with grilled foods. Whenever you cook chicken, freeze the backs and wings, so that you have them on hand when you want to make this stock.

For the bouquet garni

4 sprigs fresh flat-leaf (Italian) parsley

1 sprig fresh thyme

1 bay leaf

8 whole peppercorns

5 lb (2.5 kg) chicken backs or wings, or a combination

1 large yellow onion, peeled

1 large carrot

1 large stalk celery with leaves

2 tablespoons canola oil

2 cups (16 fl oz/500 ml) water, plus more to cover the stock ingredients

MAKES ABOUT 3 QT (3 L)

1 **Make a bouquet garni**
Wrap the parsley, thyme, bay leaf, and peppercorns in a piece of damp cheesecloth (muslin) and secure with kitchen string. Set aside.

2 **Chop the backs and wings**
If you have a heavy cleaver, chop the backs into 2- to 3-inch (5- to 7.5-cm) pieces. This will help release the gelatin from the bones. Cut the wings at the joints: Place the cleaver or a heavy knife directly in the joint (bend the wing to find the spot) and press on the top of the cleaver or knife with the heel of one palm.

3 **Roast the chicken parts**
Position an oven rack in the upper third of the oven and preheat to 425°F (220°C). (Allowing the heat to circulate underneath the pan will encourage even, deep browning of the bones.) Spread the chicken parts, overlapping them if necessary, in a very large roasting pan. A nonstick pan will work, but you want lots of browned bits to stick to the bottom of the pan—what chefs call a *fond*. Roast for 30 minutes. Using tongs, turn the pieces over and continue roasting until they are deeply browned, about 20 minutes longer.

4 **Cook the vegetables**
Meanwhile, coarsely chop the onion, carrot, and celery. Place a stockpot or large saucepan over medium-high heat. When hot, add the oil and heat until the surface just shimmers. Add the vegetables and cook, stirring occasionally, until they start to brown, 10–12 minutes.

5 Deglaze the roasting pan

Using tongs, transfer the browned chicken to the stockpot. Discard any fat in the roasting pan. Place the roasting pan over 2 burners on high heat and heat until the juices sizzle. Pour the 2 cups water into the roasting pan. Bring to a boil, scraping up the browned bits around the pan with a wooden spatula or spoon. This is known as *deglazing*.

6 Bring the stock to a boil

Pour the brown liquid into the pot, then add the bouquet garni. Add water to cover the ingredients by about 1 inch (2.5 cm); more water could dilute the flavor of the finished stock. Turn on the heat to high and bring the stock almost to a boil.

7 Simmer the stock

As soon as you see bubbles forming, reduce the heat to low. Skim off any foam from the surface with a large slotted spoon or skimmer and discard. The foam is the impurities being released from the bones and meat; if not removed, it will cloud the stock. Let the stock simmer, regularly skimming any foam from the surface, until it is full flavored, at least 3 hours and up to 6 hours. Add additional water, if necessary, to keep the ingredients just covered. Do not let the stock boil, or fat from the meat will be suspended in the stock, making it greasy.

8 Strain and defat the stock

Line a fine-mesh sieve with a damp cheesecloth and place over a large tempered glass or stainless-steel bowl. Pour the stock through the sieve and discard the solids. Let the stock stand for 5 minutes, then carefully skim the clear yellow fat from the surface with a large metal spoon. Or, if time allows, fill a large bowl partway with ice water and set the stock in the ice bath to cool to room temperature, stirring occasionally. Cover and refrigerate overnight. The fat will rise to the top and solidify, making it easy to scrape it from the surface.

9 Store the stock

Cover the stock and refrigerate it for up to 3 days, or pour into airtight containers and freeze for up to 3 months.

CHEF'S TIP

If you use stock often in small amounts, try freezing it in an ice-cube tray. After the cubes are frozen, transfer them to a locking plastic bag for longer storage. One standard ice cube melts to make about 1 tablespoon liquid.

Classic Barbecue Sauce

There are countless recipes for barbecue sauce, but this version ranks among the best. Tomato-based chili sauce and the ketchup give it a bright sweet-and-sour tang, and its mild heat can be adjusted upward with the addition of more hot-pepper sauce. The thick, clingy consistency is great for grilled food.

1 yellow onion

2 cloves garlic

2 tablespoons unsalted butter

1 cup (8 fl oz/250 ml) tomato ketchup

1 cup (8 fl oz/250 ml) American-style tomato-based chili sauce

½ cup (3½ oz/105 g) firmly packed golden brown sugar

½ cup (4 fl oz/125 ml) cider vinegar

2 tablespoons spicy brown mustard

2 tablespoons Worcestershire sauce

½ teaspoon red hot-pepper sauce

MAKES ABOUT 3 CUPS (24 FL OZ/750 ML)

1 Chop the vegetables

If you are not sure of how to cut the onion and garlic, turn to pages 32–33. Using a chef's knife, cut the onion in half lengthwise and peel each half. One at a time, place the onion halves, cut side down, on a cutting board. Alternately make a series of lengthwise cuts, parallel cuts, and then crosswise cuts to create ½-inch (12-mm) dice. Be sure to stop just short of the root end; this holds the onion together as you cut. Next, place the garlic cloves on the board, firmly press against them with the flat side of the chef's knife, and pull away and discard the papery skin. Rock the knife blade up and down and back and forth over the garlic until it is evenly chopped.

2 Cook the vegetables

Place a heavy-bottomed nonreactive saucepan over medium heat and add the butter. When the butter has melted, add the onion and cook, stirring often with a wooden spoon, until the onion is golden, about 6 minutes. Add the garlic and cook, stirring often, until the garlic is fragrant, about 1 minute.

3 Simmer the sauce

Add the ketchup, chili sauce, brown sugar, vinegar, mustard, and Worcestershire sauce. Bring to a simmer, stirring often. Reduce the heat to medium-low to keep a slow simmer. Cook uncovered, stirring often with a wooden spatula, until the sauce is thick and reduced by about one-fourth, about 30 minutes. Stir frequently to scrape up any sauce that would otherwise stick to the bottom and sides of the pan and start to scorch. Remove from the heat and stir in the hot-pepper sauce. (When using hot-pepper sauce, it is best to add it at the end of cooking, as its flavor dissipates with long simmering.)

4 **Adjust the seasonings**

Be sure to taste the sauce before using; it should have a nice, even balance of tangy, salty, sweet, and spicy, with no single flavor dominating. The flavorings are bold, so you probably won't need to adjust the seasonings. However, a little more hot-pepper sauce could lend a spicier flavor to the sauce.

5 **Use the sauce**

If you plan to use the sauce on foods on the grill, be sure to apply it only during the last 10 minutes of grilling. If it is in direct contact with the heat for longer, it may burn. If the sauce begins to scorch despite your best efforts, move the food to a cooler part of the grill so that it is not directly over the hot coals. If using a gas grill, simply reduce the heat with the thermostat. If you plan to use part of the sauce as a condiment, be sure to set some of it aside before you begin basting, to avoid cross-contamination. There are no set rules for how much sauce to use. You should add the amount that suits your taste.

6 **Store the sauce**

If you plan on storing the sauce for future use, let it cool to room temperature and transfer it to an airtight container. It can be refrigerated for up to 2 weeks. The large quantities of acids and sugar in the sauce discourage bacterial growth, so this sauce keeps well. (During outdoor-grilling season, make a double batch to store in the refrigerator.) The sauce does not freeze well, however.

CHEF'S TIP

Barbecue sauce should be applied to food only during the last 10 minutes of grilling—5 minutes on each side—or the sugar in the sauce will burn and develop undesirable charred bits on the surface of the food.

Mustard & Rosemary Barbecue Sauce

Mustard has an affinity for grilled poultry, seafood, and even pork chops. Here, whole-grain mustard provides the main flavor, but it is mellowed by Dijon mustard and accented by rosemary, wine, green onion, and garlic. This sauce goes together quickly, can be easily doubled, and keeps well in the refrigerator.

4 sprigs fresh rosemary, each 3 inches (7.5 cm) long

2 lemons

1 green (spring) onion

2 cloves garlic

½ cup (4 oz/125 g) Dijon mustard

½ cup (4 oz/125 g) whole-grain mustard

¼ cup (2 fl oz/60 ml) dry white wine such as Sauvignon Blanc

¼ cup (2 fl oz/60 ml) extra-virgin olive oil

2 tablespoons firmly packed golden brown sugar

½ teaspoon red pepper flakes

MAKES ABOUT 1¾ CUPS (14 FL OZ/430 ML)

1 Chop the rosemary

Rinse the rosemary sprigs and pat dry. With one hand, hold a rosemary sprig at the top end. Run the thumb and index finger of your other hand down the stem to strip off the leaves, which resemble pine needles. Pick any remaining leaves off the woody stem and discard the stem. Repeat with the remaining rosemary sprigs. On a cutting board, gather the rosemary leaves into a pile. Using a chef's knife, finely chop the rosemary: Hold the knife tip with one hand so that it stays on the board, then rock the heel of the knife over the pile of leaves to cut them into small pieces. You should have about 2 tablespoons. If you need help working with herbs, turn to page 35.

2 Zest the lemons

Use a rasp grater such as a fine Microplane or the small grating holes on a box grater-shredder to remove only the colored portion of the lemon peel, taking care to avoid the white pith underneath, which is bitter. Don't forget to scrape the zest from the back of the grater, where it naturally gathers. For more information on zesting lemons, turn to page 36.

3 Chop the green onion

Using the chef's knife, trim off the root end and the tough green tops of the green (spring) onion. Pull off the thin, transparent outer layer. Thinly slice the white and tender green tops. Take care to keep your fingers holding the onion safely clear of the blade. For more details on green onions, turn to page 34.

4 Mince the garlic

Place the garlic cloves on the cutting board. Using the chef's knife, firmly press against the garlic cloves with the flat side of the knife and pull away and discard the papery skins. Rock the knife blade up and down and back and forth until the garlic is minced. If you need help mincing garlic, turn to page 33.

5 Mix the sauce

In a glass or stainless-steel bowl, whisk together the Dijon and whole-grain mustards, chopped rosemary, lemon zest, sliced green onion, minced garlic, white wine, olive oil, brown sugar, and red pepper flakes until combined. Cover and let stand at room temperature for at least 30 minutes to allow the flavors to blend. If you plan to use part of the sauce as a condiment, be sure to set some of it aside before you begin basting, to avoid cross-contamination. There are no set rules for how much sauce to use. You should add the amount that suits your taste.

6 Use the sauce

To prevent foods from scorching, apply the sauce only during the last 10 minutes of grilling. If it is in direct contact with the heat for longer, it may burn. If the sauce begins to scorch despite your best efforts, move the food to a cooler part of the grill, so that it is not directly over the hot coals. If using a gas grill, simply reduce the heat with the thermostat.

7 Store the sauce

To store the sauce, transfer it to a covered container and refrigerate for up to 2 weeks. The large quantities of acids and sugar in the sauce discourage bacterial growth, so it keeps well. The sauce does not freeze well, however.

CHEF'S TIP

Herbs should be rinsed and completely dried before chopping. A quick spin in a salad spinner does the best job of removing excess water. Alternately, pat them dry with a kitchen towel or paper towel. Be sure to use a very sharp knife to ensure bright green chopped herbs. A dull knife will bruise the leaves, rather than cut them cleanly, causing them to blacken.

Key Techniques

Successful grilling, like all cooking, depends on mastering a handful of key techniques. In this chapter, you will learn how to set up a grill—both charcoal and gas—how to test foods for doneness, and how to do such everyday culinary tasks as dice an onion and toast seeds and nuts. Learn them now and you will find yourself returning to them again and again as you make the recipes in this book.

Dicing an Onion or a Shallot

1 Cut the onion in half
Using a chef's knife, cut the onion in half lengthwise, through the root end. This makes it easier to peel and gives each half a flat side for stability when you make your cuts.

2 Peel the onion
Using a paring knife, pick up the edge of the onion's papery skin and pull it away. You may also need to remove the first layer of onion if it, too, has rough or papery patches.

3 Trim the onion
Trim each end neatly, leaving some of the root intact to help hold the onion half together. Place an onion half, flat side down, on a cutting board with the root end facing away from you.

4 Cut the onion lengthwise
Hold the onion securely on both sides. Using the chef's knife, make a series of lengthwise cuts, as thick as you want the final dice to be. Do not cut all the way through the root end.

5 Cut the onion horizontally
Spread your fingers across the onion to help keep it together. Turn the knife blade parallel to the cutting board and make a series of horizontal cuts as thick as you want the final dice to be.

6 Cut the onion crosswise
Still holding the onion together with your fingers, cut it crosswise to dice it. Dicing an onion in this methodical way gives you pieces that cook evenly.

Working with Garlic

1 Loosen the garlic peel

Using the flat side of a chef's knife, firmly press against the clove. If you plan to mince the garlic, it's fine to smash it. If you are slicing it, use light pressure to keep the clove intact.

2 Peel and halve the clove

The pressure from the knife will cause the garlic peel to split. Grasp the peel with your fingers, pull it away, and then discard it. Cut the garlic clove in half lengthwise to make flat sides.

TROUBLESHOOTING

You may see a small green sprout running through the middle of a garlic clove. If left in, it could impart a bitter flavor to the dish. Use the tip of a paring knife to pop out the sprout, and then discard it.

3 Cut the garlic into slices

Working with half the clove at a time, use the knife to cut the garlic into very thin slices. Use the slices, or, if chopping or mincing, gather the slices in a pile in the center of the board.

4 Chop the garlic

Rest the fingertips of one hand on top of the tip of the knife. Move the heel of the knife in a rhythmic up-and-down motion over the garlic slices until evenly chopped.

5 Mince the garlic

Stop occasionally to clean the knife of garlic bits and gather them in a compact pile on the board. Continue to chop until the garlic pieces are very fine, or *minced*.

Working with Green Onions

1 Trim the onions

Using a chef's knife, trim off the roots and tough green tops of the green (spring) onions.

Working with Chiles

1 Quarter the chile

Many cooks wear a disposable latex glove on the hand that touches the chile to prevent irritation from its potent oils. Using a paring knife, cut the chile in half, then in quarters.

2 Remove the seeds and ribs

Cut away the seeds, ribs, and stem from each chile quarter. *Capsaicin*, the compound that makes chiles hot, is concentrated in these areas; removing them lessens the heat.

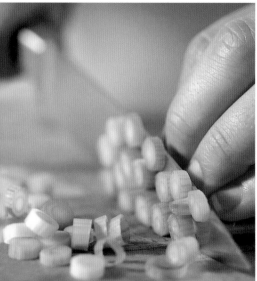

2 Slice the onions crosswise

If the recipe calls for thinly sliced green onions, line up the trimmed ends and slice the onions crosswise. To mince the onions, rock the heel of the knife over the slices.

3 Cut the quarters into strips

Place the quarters, cut side up, on the cutting board. Cut into narrow slices about ⅛ inch (3 mm) thick. Take care not to pierce the glove.

4 Mince the strips

Line up the chile strips and cut them crosswise at ⅛-inch (3-mm) intervals. Rest your fingertips on the top of the tip of the knife and rock the heel of the knife over the pieces to mince them.

Working with Fresh Ginger

TECHNIQUE

1 Peel the ginger

Using a vegetable peeler, peel away the papery brown skin from the ginger to reveal the light flesh underneath.

2 Chop the ginger

Using a chef's knife, cut the peeled ginger into disks and then cut the disks into strips. Cut the strips crosswise into small pieces. To mince the pieces, rock the heel of the knife over them.

Chopping & Mincing Herbs

TECHNIQUE

1 Separate the leaves

After rinsing and patting dry the herb, use your fingers to pluck the leaves from the sprigs and discard the stems. Gather the leaves together into a pile on a cutting board.

2 Chop the herb

Rest your fingertips on the top of the tip of a chef's knife and rock the heel of the knife over the board to chop the leaves. If the recipe calls for a coarsely chopped herb, chop it only briefly.

3 Mince the herb

If the recipe calls for a minced herb, regather the leaves into a compact pile, cleaning the herbs off the knife and adding them to the pile, and continue to chop into very fine pieces.

4 Transfer the leaves

To remove chopped or minced leaves from the board, use the flat side of the knife to scoop them up. Then run your finger carefully along the flat side of the blade to slide them into a dish.

Zesting & Juicing Citrus

1 Zest the lemon

If you are zesting and juicing a lemon, zest it first. Use a fine rasp grater or the grating teeth on a box grater-shredder to remove only the colored peel, not the bitter white pith.

2 Clean off the grater

Don't forget to scrape all the zest from the back of the grater, where some of it naturally gathers.

Toasting Nuts or Seeds

1 Toast the nuts or seeds in a pan

Place the nuts or seeds in a dry frying pan over medium heat. Stir them frequently to keep them from burning.

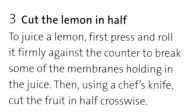

3 Cut the lemon in half

To juice a lemon, first press and roll it firmly against the counter to break some of the membranes holding in the juice. Then, using a chef's knife, cut the fruit in half crosswise.

4 Juice the lemon

To extract as much juice as possible, use a citrus reamer to pierce the membranes as you squeeze. Catch the juice in a bowl and strain to remove any seeds before using.

2 Let the nuts or seeds cool

As soon as the nuts or seeds are golden, after 2–3 minutes, transfer them to a plate so they don't continue to cook in the pan. They will become a little crisper as they cool.

Trimming a Roast

1 Trim the fat from the roast
Using a rigid boning knife or a chef's knife, begin to cut away the external fat on the surface of the roast. Cut the fat off in long, uniform strips to ensure an even layer.

2 Leave on a thin layer of fat
Leave a layer of fat ¼–½ inch (6–12 mm) thick on the roast. This small amount will help to flavor and moisturize the meat as it cooks. Discard the fat you removed.

Trimming a Steak

1 Trim the fat
Using a rigid boning knife or a chef's knife, trim away most of the external fat around the edge of the steak. For rib-eye steaks, also cut out the nugget of fat that's often found in the center.

TROUBLESHOOTING
Steaks can curl when cooked over high heat. To prevent this, use a rigid boning knife or a paring knife to *score* the edges: cut 2 or 3 shallow, evenly spaced slashes in the surrounding fat.

2 Leave on a thin layer of fat
Leave a layer of fat ¼–½ inch (6–12 mm) thick on the steak. This small amount will help to flavor and moisturize the meat as it cooks. Discard the fat you removed.

3 Put the steaks on a plate
As you trim the steaks, put them on a plate in a single layer. If you stack them, they will pull juices from each other.

Using a Chimney Starter

1 Stuff with newspaper

Remove the grill grate. Turn the chimney starter upside down on the fire bed and stuff with newspaper.

Direct-Heat Charcoal Grilling

1 Pour the coals into the fire bed

Protecting your hand with an oven mitt, turn the chimney starter over to dump the coals into the fire bed.

2 Add the coals

Turn the chimney starter right side up on the fire bed, keeping the newspaper secure in the bottom. Add coals just to the top. I like a mixture of briquettes and hardwood.

3 Ignite the newspaper

Using a long match or gas wand, ignite the newspaper. The flames will rise upward and ignite the coals. Leave the chimney starter in place until the coals are covered with white ash.

2 Arrange the coals in heat zones

Using tongs, arrange the coals 2 or 3 layers deep in one-third of the fire bed and 1 or 2 layers deep in another third, leaving the remaining third free of coals.

Indirect-Heat Charcoal Grilling

1 Arrange the coals

Using tongs, arrange the coals in 2 equal piles on 2 sides of the grill, leaving the center free of coals.

2 Position a drip pan

Place an aluminum foil pan in the area between the coals to catch the dripping fat, creating a cool zone for the grill. Add enough water to fill the pan halfway up the sides.

Setting Up a Gas Grill

1 Starting a gas grill

Following the manufacturer's directions for your grill, secure the gas line to the fuel tank.

2 Lighting the gas grill

Turn the gas knob right, or to the "open" position. To start the flow of gas, open the lid, turn the burners on, and depress the ignition switch. Adjust the heat level as directed in the recipe.

Oiling the Grate

1 Dip rolled paper towels in oil

Pour oil into a small container. Fold 4 paper towels in half, then roll them up tightly into a cylinder. Using tongs, grasp the rolled towels and dip them into the oil.

2 Brush the grate with the towels

Still using the tongs, brush the grill rack with the oiled towels. The oil keeps food from sticking and makes cleanup easier.

Using Wood Chips on a Charcoal Grill

1 Soak wood chips in water

Put the wood chips in a large bowl with water to cover and soak for at least 30 minutes.

Using Wood Chips on a Gas Grill

1 Divide the wood chips

Soak the wood chips as directed for the charcoal grill, setting aside 1 handful of dry chips. The dry chips will be easier to ignite than the wet wood chips.

2 Add dry chips to a smoker box

If you have a smoker box, usually made from cast iron, remove the vented cover and add the reserved dry chips to the bottom part.

2 Add the wood chips to the coals

Sprinkle the soaked wood chips directly onto the hot coals. The wet chips will smolder, releasing their aromatic smoke slowly, without burning too quickly.

3 Or, add dry chips to a foil packet

Fold a 12-by-16-inch (30-by-40-cm) piece of aluminum foil in half and place the dry chips in the center. Fold over and crimp the three open sides. Tear open the top to reveal the chips.

4 Ignite the wood chips

Place the dry chips, in the box or packet, directly over a heat element and let heat until they ignite. Add a handful of the soaked chips to the dry chips to generate a head of smoke.

Creating Crosshatch Grill Marks

Cleaning the Grill

1 Line up the steaks
Place the steaks on the grill, making sure they all face the same direction. Remember the order you put them on the grill, so you know which one to turn first.

2 Rotate the steaks
Leave the steaks undisturbed for 1–1½ minutes to develop good grill marks. Using tongs, rotate each steak 90 degrees and continue cooking undisturbed for 1–1½ minutes.

1 Scrub the grill with a wire brush
After cooking, while the grill is still hot, use a long-handled wire brush to scrape off any food particles that are stuck on the grill grate. This is an important step in grill maintenance.

3 Turn over the steaks
Starting with the first steak, turn over the steaks, again lining them up in the same direction. You'll notice the square-shaped cross-hatching you created by rotating the steaks.

4 Crosshatch the second side
Leave the steaks undisturbed for 1–1½ minutes to develop good grill marks. Using tongs, again rotate each steak 90 degrees and continue cooking for 1–1½ minutes.

2 Close the grill cover
Be sure that the burners are off on a gas grill and close the grill cover. On a charcoal grill, close the vents on the side of the grill to inhibit the oxygen flow and cause the coals to burn out.

Testing Doneness by Temperature

1 Test a steak for doneness

Insert an instant-read thermometer horizontally into the center of the steak. Be sure not to touch any bone.

2 Test a roast for doneness

Insert the thermometer into the thickest part of the roast, away from any bone. Turn to page 17 for information about the doneness temperatures for beef.

Testing Doneness Visually

1 Cut into the steak

Use a paring knife to make a small cut in the thickest part near the center of the meat (away from the bone, if present). Pull the meat apart and note its color.

2 Rare steak

Beef cooked to the rare stage is deep red at the center and very juicy.

3 Medium-rare steak

Beef cooked to the medium-rare stage is deep pink in the center. It will be firmer than rare beef but still juicy.

4 Medium steak

Beef cooked to the medium stage will be light pink in the center. The texture is firm and compact.

Testing Chicken

1 Test chicken by temperature
Insert an instant-read thermometer into the thigh, away from the bone. The temperature should be at least 170°F (77°C). The temperature will also rise 5°–10°F (3°–6°C) as it rests.

TROUBLESHOOTING
If you cut into the chicken and it releases pink juices, it is undercooked. Return it to the grill until the juices run clear yellow, indicating the chicken is cooked through.

Testing Pork

1 Test pork by temperature
Insert an instant-read thermometer into the thickest part of the meat. The temperature should be at least 150°F (65°C) for medium. The temperature will also rise 5°–10°F (3°–6°C) as it rests.

2 Test pork by sight
Using a chef's knife, cut into slices ¼–½ inch (6–12 mm) thick. Pork cooked to the medium stage should be light pink in the center. It will be firm but still juicy.

Testing Fish

1 Test fish by sight
Using the tip of a paring knife, slice into the flesh of the fish. Unless you are cooking fish to the rare stage, the interior should be barely opaque but still very moist.

TROUBLESHOOTING
If you overcook fish, it will flake apart when you cut into it. To prevent overcooking, test for doneness periodically with the tip of a paring knife as shown above.

Direct-Heat Grilling

Here, you will see how direct-heat grilling imparts a crisp surface and juicy center to such long-standing grill favorites as burgers and steaks. You will also discover how the heat of the grill helps to intensify the spices and other seasonings used in marinades and sauces and pass along their flavors to the grilled foods. There are some surprises here, too, including grilled mussels and stuffed trout.

Classic Hamburgers

A burger fresh off the grill, with a crusty, deep brown exterior and juicy interior, is an icon of outdoor cooking. For the best flavor and texture, chop the beef at home, rather than buy it already ground from your butcher. Partially freezing the meat and using a food processor make this step easy.

1 Cut up and partially freeze the beef

Put the beef round on a cutting board. Using a chef's knife, cut the meat into slices about ¾ inch (2 cm) thick. Next, cut the slices into ¾-inch-wide strips. Finally, line up a few strips at a time and cut them crosswise into ¾-inch chunks. Without crowding, spread the chunks in a single layer on a rimmed baking sheet. (I like to line it with waxed paper for easy cleanup). Put the baking sheet in the freezer and freeze until the meat begins to form ice crystals around the edges, about 40 minutes. This step firms up the meat and makes it easier to chop in the food processor.

2 Chop the beef

Fit an impeccably clean food processor with the metal blade. Transfer half of the partially frozen beef chunks to the food processor. Pulse the processor about 20 times, or until the beef is very finely chopped into pieces less than ⅛ inch (3 mm) square. Remove the blade and transfer the chopped beef to a large, clean bowl. Repeat to process the remaining beef.

3 Season and mix the beef

Your hands are the most efficient tools for mixing chopped beef. Wash your hands well with soap and hot water before mixing the beef, and then again before touching anything else. This will discourage contaminating food or kitchen surfaces and utensils with potentially harmful bacteria. Sprinkle the salt and pepper evenly over the beef. Using clean hands, once again mix the beef and seasonings until just combined. Handling the meat too much will melt the fat and make for an unpleasantly dense burger, so use a light touch. Once again, wash your hands well with soap and hot water. ❯

1½ lb (750 g) boneless beef round

1 teaspoon salt

½ teaspoon freshly ground pepper

4 hamburger buns, split

Canola oil for coating the grill grate

For the accompaniments

Onion slices

Tomato slices

Dill pickle slices

Cooked bacon slices

Tender leaf lettuce leaves

Good-quality tomato ketchup

Good-quality mayonnaise

Dijon or whole-grain mustard

MAKES 4 SERVINGS

CHEF'S TIP

Do not attempt to chop the beef in the food processor without freezing it first. If you do, the fat will emulsify with the meat, affecting the texture and flavor of the finished patties.

4>>

5 >

4 Form the patties

Line a rimmed baking sheet with waxed paper. Moisten your clean hands (this will prevent the meat from sticking to your hands) and divide the beef into 4 equal portions. Moistening your hands each time, lightly pat each portion into a patty 4–4½ inches (10–11.5 cm) in diameter and about ¾ inch (2 cm) thick. Again, avoid overhandling or compacting the meat. Place the meat patties on the lined baking sheet, cover with plastic wrap, and refrigerate for at least 2 hours or up to 24 hours. This will allow the seasonings to permeate the meat, giving the burgers the most flavorful results. Remove the patties from the refrigerator 30 minutes before grilling.

SHORTCUT

If you don't want to chop the beef yourself, you can substitute 1½ lb (750 g) purchased ground (minced) round for the boneless beef round and start the recipe at step 3.

5 Prepare the grill

If you need help setting up a grill, turn to pages 38–39. About 20 minutes before you start cooking, prepare a charcoal or gas grill with 2 areas of high heat and 1 cooler area: **IF YOU ARE USING A CHARCOAL GRILL,** first remove the grill grate and set it aside. Next, ignite the briquettes and/or charcoal using a chimney starter and let them burn until they are covered with white ash. Then pour the coals into the fire bed. Finally, using long-handled tongs, spread the hot coals 2 or 3 layers deep in one-third of the fire bed and 1 or 2 layers deep in another third of the fire bed, leaving the remaining third free of coals. Replace the grill grate in its slots. **IF YOU ARE USING A GAS GRILL,** turn on all of the heat elements as high as they will go. **FOR EITHER TYPE OF GRILL,** place a serving platter near the grill to warm from its heat, or warm it in a 200°F (95°C) oven. You will use it to hold the patties and buns after they are cooked. (Never serve cooked meat on the same plate that the raw meat was on, as you could contaminate the cooked meat with bacteria.) Scrub the grill grate with a wire brush to remove any traces of food. Then, lightly rub the grill grate with paper towels coated with canola oil. For more details on oiling the grill grate, see page 39. >

6 Grill the patties

Before grilling, test the grill temperature. **IF YOU ARE USING A CHARCOAL GRILL,** hold your hand about 4 inches (10 cm) above the fire. If you can count only to 1 before pulling your hand away (very high heat), the coals are ready. **IF YOU ARE USING A GAS GRILL,** leave 1 or 2 heat elements on high and turn the other heat element off. The temperature should reach 500°F (260°C) before you begin to cook. **FOR EITHER TYPE OF GRILL,** place the patties over the hottest part of the grill, and cover, if desired (see page 9). Grill until the undersides of the patties are crisp and browned, 3–4 minutes, rotating them with a long-handled spatula 90 degrees after 1½–2 minutes if you desire cross-hatching. For more details on cross-hatching, turn to page 41. Turn over the patties, cover again, and grill until done to your liking, about 4 minutes more for medium, again rotating the patties by 90 degrees after 2 minutes for cross-hatching. If the dripping juices cause flare-ups, move the patties to the cooler area of the grill. Do not turn them over more than once, to ensure a deeply browned crust.

CHEF'S TIP

Resist the urge to press down on the patties with the spatula to speed the cooking. You will lose precious juices and encourage flare-ups.

7 Check the patties for doneness

Insert an instant-read thermometer into the center of a patty. It should register 145°F (63°C) for medium. If not, let cook for 1 minute longer and check again. For more details on testing for doneness, turn to page 42.

8 Toast the buns and serve the burgers

About 1 minute before the patties are done, place the buns, cut sides down, at the edge of the grill until lightly toasted. Transfer the toasted buns to the warmed serving platter and assemble the patties in the buns. Serve right way.

9 Clean and maintain the grill for the next use

While the grill is still hot, use a sturdy grill brush to clean the grill grate. **IF YOU ARE USING A CHARCOAL GRILL,** cover it and let the coals burn out completely. **IF YOU ARE USING A GAS GRILL,** turn off the heat elements, seal the propane tank, and close the grill cover.

Serving ideas

A grilled burger is the perfect canvas for a variety of toppings, limited only by your imagination. For the best results, keep the choices simple: grilled onions, melted Cheddar cheese, freshly made guacamole. Consider different types of breads, too. Ciabatta buns, whole-grain rolls, pita rounds, or even sliced country bread are all good choices. For the most satisfying results, make sure the burgers are sizzling hot off the grill.

Grilled onions (top left)

Follow the instructions on pages 121–24 for grilled onions. Remove them from the aluminum foil and place them directly on the grill grate until the edges of the slices are slightly charred.

Guacamole (left)

Halve and pit an avocado. Using a spoon, scoop the flesh from the skin, break it into small chunks with a fork, and season with salt, pepper, lime juice, and, if desired, minced jalapeño.

Cheeseburgers (above)

Thinly slice Cheddar cheese. Place 2 slices on each patty about 2–3 minutes before you remove the patties from the grill.

Burger Variations

Using what you have learned making Classic Hamburgers (page 47)—how to chop your own meat, the need to allow time for the seasonings to permeate the beef, taking care not to handle the patties too much—you can now prepare juicy burgers with lamb, turkey, chicken, salmon, and tuna. Because burgers made from poultry and fish are lean and thus more apt to dry out on the grill, you will need to use a medium fire and to add ingredients to hold in the moisture. I've included a vegetarian burger, too, made with portobello mushroom caps. Serve each burger with your choice of accompaniments. Each variation makes 4 servings.

Blue Cheese Burgers

Sandwich the pungent blue cheese between two thin layers of ground beef before grilling, so that the cheese is a tasty surprise.

Follow the recipe for Classic Hamburgers (page 47). In step 4, divide the chopped beef mixture into 8 portions. Shape into 8 thin patties, each about 4 inches (10 cm) in diameter.

Cut 2 oz (60 g) blue cheese, such as Danish blue or Roquefort, into 4 slices. Top 4 of the patties with 1 slice of the cheese, leaving a ½-inch (12-mm) border around the edge of each patty. Cover each cheese-topped patty with the 4 remaining patties, then lightly pat them together to enclose the blue cheese entirely. Cover and refrigerate for 2–24 hours. Remove from the refrigerator 30 minutes before grilling.

Continue with the recipe to grill the patties. During the last minute of grilling, put 4 split hamburger buns at the edge of the grill and grill until lightly toasted. Assemble the patties in the buns and serve right away on a warmed platter.

Provençal Lamb Burgers

Serve with aioli, made from ⅔ cup (5 fl oz/160 ml) prepared mayonnaise mixed with 2 finely minced garlic cloves.

Cut 1½ lb (750 g) well-trimmed boneless lamb shoulder or leg into ¾-inch (2-cm) chunks (or use 1½ lb/750 g ground lamb). Spread the chunks in a single layer on a baking sheet and freeze for about 40 minutes. In 2 batches, pulse the lamb in a food processor until finely chopped and transfer to a bowl. Add ⅓ cup (2 oz/60 g) finely chopped kalamata olives, 1 teaspoon crumbled dried rosemary, 1 teaspoon crumbled dried oregano, 1 teaspoon salt, and ½ teaspoon freshly ground pepper.

Form the lamb mixture into four 4½-by-¾-inch (11.5-by-2-cm) patties. Cover and refrigerate for 2–24 hours. Remove from the refrigerator 30 minutes before grilling.

Prepare a charcoal or gas grill for direct grilling over medium heat. Oil the grill grate. Grill the lamb patties, turning once, until they are done to your liking, 7–8 minutes total for medium.

Top each patty with roasted red pepper (capsicum) pieces on 4 toasted pita bread rounds. Serve right away on a warmed platter.

Turkey Burgers

Ground turkey that is a mix of white and dark meat is the best choice for turkey burgers. The breast meat is too lean to withstand the heat of a grill.

Put 1½ lb (750 g) ground (minced) turkey in a large bowl. Add 3 tablespoons Classic Barbecue Sauce (page 26), 3 tablespoons dried bread crumbs, 1 teaspoon salt, and ½ teaspoon freshly ground pepper and mix gently with your hands.

Form the turkey mixture into four 4½-by-¾-inch (11.5-by-2-cm) patties. Cover and refrigerate for 30 minutes– 2 hours. Remove from the refrigerator 30 minutes before grilling.

Prepare a charcoal or gas grill for direct grilling over medium heat. Oil the grill grate. Grill the turkey patties, turning once, until they feel firm and are medium-well done, about 10 minutes total. During the last 2 minutes of grilling, brush the tops of the patties with about ⅓ cup (3 fl oz/80 ml) Classic Barbecue Sauce (page 26).

During the last minute of grilling, put 4 split hamburger buns at the edge of the grill and grill until lightly toasted. Assemble the patties in the buns and serve right away on a warmed platter.

Salmon-Mustard Burgers

To make a complementary condiment for this burger, mix ½ cup (4 fl oz/125 ml) mayonnaise with 3 tablespoons whole-grain mustard.

Cut 1½ lb (750 g) skinless salmon fillet into ¾-inch (2-cm) chunks, but do not freeze them. Transfer the fish to a food processor fitted with the metal blade. Pulse the salmon about 10 times, or until chopped into pieces about ¼ inch (6 mm) square. Add 3 tablespoons dried bread crumbs, 2 tablespoons mayonnaise, 1 tablespoon whole-grain mustard, the grated zest of ½ lemon, ½ teaspoon salt, and ¼ teaspoon freshly ground pepper. Pulse about 5 more times, or until the ingredients are evenly combined and the salmon is very finely chopped. Transfer to a bowl.

Lightly form the salmon mixture into four 4½-by-¾-inch (11.5-by-2-cm) patties. Cover and refrigerate for 30 minutes–2 hours. Remove from the refrigerator 30 minutes before grilling.

Prepare a charcoal or gas grill for direct grilling over medium heat. Oil the grill grate. Grill the salmon patties, turning once, until they begin to feel firm in the center (they will not get deeply browned like beef burgers), about 6 minutes total for medium-rare; do not overcook.

During the last minute of grilling, put 4 split hamburger buns at the edge of the grill and grill until lightly toasted. Assemble the patties in the buns and serve right away on a warmed platter.

Asian Tuna Burgers

The bold flavor of tuna takes well to Asian flavors, such as ginger, hoisin sauce, and sesame oil. For a Chinese-style condiment, mix ½ cup (4 fl oz/125 ml) tomato ketchup with 2 tablespoons hoisin sauce.

Cut 1½ lb (750 g) skinless tuna fillet into ¾-inch (2-cm) chunks, but do not freeze them. Transfer the fish to a food processor fitted with the metal blade. Pulse the tuna about 10 times, until chopped into pieces about ¼ inch (6 mm) square. Add 3 tablespoons dried bread crumbs, 1 tablespoon peeled and minced fresh ginger, 2 tablespoons hoisin sauce, 1 tablespoon Asian sesame oil, ½ teaspoon salt, and ¼ teaspoon freshly ground pepper. Pulse about 5 more times, or until the ingredients are evenly combined and the tuna is very finely chopped. Transfer to a bowl.

Lightly form the tuna mixture into four 4½-by-¾-inch (11.5-by-2-cm) patties. Cover and refrigerate for 30 minutes–2 hours. Remove the patties from the refrigerator 30 minutes before grilling.

Prepare a charcoal or gas grill for direct grilling over medium heat. Oil the grill grate. Grill the tuna patties, turning once, until they begin to feel firm in the center (they will not get deeply browned like beef burgers), about 6 minutes total for medium-rare; do not overcook.

During the last minute of grilling, put 4 split hamburger buns at the edge of the grill and grill until lightly toasted. Assemble the patties in the buns and serve right away on a warmed platter.

Mushroom Burgers

Marinated and grilled portobello mushrooms make wonderful burgers. They're also the perfect option for nonmeat eaters at a backyard cookout.

Make a marinade: In a small glass bowl, whisk together ½ cup (4 fl oz/125 ml) dry red wine, 2 tablespoons extra-virgin olive oil, 1 tablespoon balsamic vinegar, 1 tablespoon soy sauce, ¾ teaspoon dried *herbes de Provence*, ½ minced garlic clove, and ⅛ teaspoon red pepper flakes; set aside.

Remove the stems from 4 portobello mushrooms, each about 5 inches (13 cm) in diameter. Cut the stems in half lengthwise. Wipe the caps and stems clean with a damp kitchen towel. Place in a glass bowl or locking plastic bag and add the marinade. Cover the bowl or seal the bag and let stand at room temperature for 15 minutes–1 hour.

Prepare a charcoal or gas grill for direct grilling over medium heat. Oil the grill grate.

Remove the mushroom caps and stems from the marinade and shake off the excess. Grill the caps and stems, turning once, until they are tender and browned, 6–8 minutes total. During the last minute of grilling, put 4 thinly sliced pieces country bread at the edge of the grill and grill until lightly toasted.

Assemble the mushroom caps and stems on 4 of the toasted bread slices, top with 16 arugula (rocket) leaves, dividing evenly, and the remaining bread slices. Serve right away on a warmed platter.

Grilled T-Bone Steaks with Thyme-Garlic Paste

The high heat of the grill helps create the dark brown exterior that is the signature of a great steak. Tender T-bones, which include portions of both the tenderloin and short loin, should be simply prepared so that their beef flavor can shine. A marinade could be overpowering, but this fresh herb and garlic paste is the perfect accent.

For the thyme-garlic paste

About 25 sprigs fresh thyme, about 2 inches (5 cm) long

3 cloves garlic

1 teaspoon salt

3 tablespoons extra-virgin olive oil

¾ teaspoon freshly ground pepper

Canola oil for coating the grill grate

4 T-bone steaks, each 12–14 oz (375–440 g) and about 1 inch (2.5 cm) thick

MAKES 4 SERVINGS

CHEF'S TIP
The T-bone steak is actually two steaks in one. It includes a section of the tenderloin on one side and has a section of the top loin, also very tender, on the other side.

1 **Make the thyme-garlic paste**
Rinse the thyme sprigs and pat dry. With one hand, hold a thyme sprig at the top (nonstem) end. Run the thumb and index finger of your other hand down the stem to strip off the leaves, then discard the stem. Repeat with the remaining thyme sprigs. On a cutting board, gather the thyme leaves into a pile. Using a chef's knife, rock it rhythmically over the thyme leaves until they are finely minced. You should have about 3 tablespoons. If you are not sure of how to do this, turn to page 35. Next, make the garlic paste: Place the garlic cloves on the cutting board, firmly press against them with the flat side of the chef's knife, and pull away and discard the papery skins. Rock the knife blade back and forth and up and down to chop the garlic. Sprinkle the garlic with the salt and continue chopping until it is minced. Using the broad, flat side of the knife, smear the garlic until it is mashed into a paste. Add the thyme, garlic, olive oil, and pepper to a small bowl and mix until thoroughly blended. For more information about working with garlic, turn to page 33.

2 **Coat the steaks with the herb paste**
Trim the steaks, leaving ¼–½ inch (6–12mm) of fat around the edges. If you need help trimming steaks, turn to page 37. Using a small spatula, spread the paste over both sides of each steak, dividing it evenly. Transfer to a rimmed baking sheet lined with waxed paper. Cover with plastic wrap and let stand at room temperature while preparing the grill, up to 30 minutes.

3 **Prepare the grill**
If you need help setting up a grill, turn to pages 38–39. About 20 minutes before you start cooking, prepare a charcoal or gas grill with 2 areas of high heat and 1 cooler area: **IF YOU ARE USING A CHARCOAL GRILL,** first remove the grill grate and set it aside. Next, ignite the briquettes and/or charcoal using a chimney starter and let them burn until they are covered with white ash. Then, pour the coals into the fire bed. Finally, using long-handled tongs, spread the hot coals 2 or 3 layers deep in one-third of the fire bed and 1 or 2 layers deep in another third of the fire bed, leaving the remaining third free of coals. Replace the grill grate. **IF YOU ARE USING A GAS GRILL,** turn on all of the heat elements as high as they will go. **FOR EITHER TYPE OF GRILL,** place a serving platter near the grill to warm from its heat, or warm it in a 200°F (95°C) oven. It will hold the cooked steaks. Scrub the grill grate with a grill brush to remove any traces of food. Then, lightly rub the grate with paper towels coated with canola oil; for more details, turn to page 39.

4 Grill the steaks

Before grilling, test the grill temperature. **IF YOU ARE USING A CHARCOAL GRILL,** hold your hand about 4 inches (10 cm) above the fire. If you can count only to 1 before pulling your hand away (very high heat), the coals are ready. **IF YOU ARE USING A GAS GRILL,** leave 1 or 2 heat elements on high and turn the other heat element on low. The temperature should reach 500°F (260°C) before you begin to cook. **FOR EITHER TYPE OF GRILL,** place the steaks over the hottest part of the grill, and cover, if desired (see page 9). Grill the steaks, turning once, until they are done to your liking, 6–8 minutes for medium-rare. If you want cross-hatching on your steaks, use long-handled tongs to rotate them 90 degrees after 1½–2 minutes of cooking on each side. If you need help creating cross-hatching, turn to page 41. If the dripping juices cause flare-ups, move the steaks to the cooler part of the grill, where the juices are less likely to ignite, and continue to cook.

5 Check the steaks for doneness

Insert an instant-read thermometer horizontally into the center of the steak away from the bone (the bone will skew the temperature), or, if necessary, cut into the steak near the bone. At medium-rare, the thermometer should read 140°F (60°C) or the color should be deep pink. If the steaks are not ready, cover the grill, let them cook for 1–2 minutes longer, and test again. To find out more about checking meat for doneness, turn to page 42.

6 Let the steaks rest

When the steaks are done to your liking, transfer them to the warmed serving platter and let rest for 3–5 minutes. This brief rest allows the juices to redistribute throughout the meat. The temperature of the steak will also rise about 5°F (3°C). If cut too soon, the juices will leach out and the color inside will be uneven.

7 Clean and maintain the grill for the next use

While the meat is resting, use a sturdy grill brush to clean the still-hot grill grate. **IF YOU ARE USING A CHARCOAL GRILL,** cover it and let the coals burn out completely. **IF YOU ARE USING A GAS GRILL,** turn off the heat elements, seal the propane tank, and close the grill cover.

8 Serve the steaks

Serve the steaks right away on the warmed serving platter. Provide serrated steak knives for easy cutting.

T-Bone Steak Variations

Now that you have mastered Grilled T-Bone Steaks with Thyme-Garlic Paste (page 54), you can use your newfound skills—how to make an herb paste, how to trim a steak, how to check for doneness, the importance of letting steaks rest before serving—to grill such similar, also tender cuts as center-cut veal, pork, and lamb loin chops. Each of these meats is matched with a complementary herb—rosemary and lamb, sage and pork, *herbes de Provence* and veal—to show off its flavor. Garlic, which goes well with almost any type of grilled meat, is included in all the pastes. Each variation makes 4 servings.

Lamb Chops with Rosemary-Garlic Paste

Lamb loin chops are thick, so they need a longer cooking time than T-bone steaks. Fresh mint can be substituted for the rosemary if you prefer.

Make the rosemary-garlic paste: In a small bowl, mix together 2 tablespoons finely chopped fresh rosemary, 3 garlic cloves mashed with ¾ teaspoon salt, 2 tablespoons extra-virgin olive oil, and ½ teaspoon freshly ground pepper.

Spread the paste over both sides of 8 lamb loin chops, each about 4½ oz (140 g) and 1½ inches (4 cm) thick. Let stand for 30 minutes.

Prepare a charcoal or gas grill for direct grilling over high heat. Oil the grill grate.

Grill the chops over the hottest part of the grill, turning once, until both sides are nicely browned, about 2 minutes per side. Move to the cooler area of the grill and cover. Continue cooking, turning once, until the chops are done to your liking, about 6 minutes more for medium-rare.

Let the chops rest for 3–5 minutes, then serve right away on warmed plates.

Pork Chops with Sage-Garlic Paste

Pork chops that are grilled to medium will have the best flavor and texture.

Make the sage-garlic paste: In a small bowl, mix together ⅓ cup (½ oz/15 g) finely chopped fresh sage, 2 garlic cloves mashed with 1½ teaspoons salt, 6 tablespoons (3 fl oz/90 ml) extra-virgin olive oil, and ¾ teaspoon freshly ground pepper.

Spread the paste over both sides of 8 center-cut pork loin chops, each about ½ lb (250 g) and 1 inch (2.5 cm) thick. Let stand for 30 minutes.

Prepare a charcoal or gas grill for direct grilling over high heat. Oil the grill grate.

Grill the chops over the hottest part of the grill, turning once, until both sides are nicely browned, about 2 minutes per side. Move to the cooler area of the grill and cover. Continue cooking, turning once, until the chops are done to your liking, about 8 minutes more for medium.

Let the chops rest for 3–5 minutes, then serve right away on warmed plates.

Veal Chops with Provençal Paste

Herbes de Provence, a mixture of dried thyme, rosemary, basil, and other herbs, provides aromatic notes to enhance the delicate veal.

Make the herb-garlic paste: In a small bowl, mix together 2 tablespoons *herbes de Provence,* 1 garlic clove mashed with 1½ teaspoons salt, 2 tablespoons extra-virgin olive oil, and ½ teaspoon freshly ground pepper.

Spread the paste over both sides of 4 center-cut veal loin chops, each about 10 oz (315 g) and 1 inch (2.5 cm) thick. Let stand for 30 minutes.

Prepare a charcoal or gas grill for direct grilling over high heat. Oil the grill grate.

Grill the chops over the hottest part of the grill, turning once, until nicely browned, about 2 minutes per side. Move to the cooler area of the grill and cover. Continue cooking, turning once, until the chops are done to your liking, about 8 minutes more for medium.

Let the chops rest for 3–5 minutes, then serve right away on warmed plates.

Carne Asada

Latin American carne asada, or "grilled meat," typically starts with tough but tasty flank steak, which is tenderized, moisturized, and flavored with a bold marinade. On the grill, it becomes a rich medium brown on the outside and juicy and pink on the inside. When served, it is sliced across the grain, further enhancing its tenderness.

1 Make the marinade

Fit a food processor with the metal blade. With the machine running, drop the garlic through the feed tube to chop finely. Turn off the machine, add the cilantro, and pulse a few times until the cilantro is coarsely chopped. With the machine running, add the beer, lime zest, lime juice, olive oil, chili powder, cumin, oregano, ground chipotle (if using), and salt. (Chipotle will lend a smoky flavor.) You will have about 1½ cups (12 fl oz/375 ml) marinade.

2 Marinate the steak

Put the steak and marinade in a shallow ceramic or glass dish just large enough to hold the steak. Do not use metal, which may react with the acids in the marinade and impart off flavors. Cover the dish tightly with plastic wrap. (Alternatively, put the steak and marinade in a large locking plastic bag. These plastic bags are good for marinating because they allow a lot of contact between the food and the marinade.) Refrigerate the steak and marinade for at least 4 hours or up to 24 hours, turning the meat occasionally to ensure that the marinade touches as much of its surface area as possible. Remove the steak in its marinade from the refrigerator 1 hour before grilling. Bringing the steak to room temperature before grilling helps it to cook more evenly.

3 Prepare the grill

If you need help setting up a grill, turn to pages 38–39. About 20 minutes before you start cooking, prepare a charcoal or gas grill with 2 areas of high heat and 1 cooler area: **IF YOU ARE USING A CHARCOAL GRILL,** first remove the grill grate and set it aside. Next, ignite the briquettes and/or charcoal using a chimney starter and let them burn until they are covered with white ash. Then, pour the coals into the fire bed. Finally, using long-handled tongs, spread the hot coals 2 or 3 layers deep in one-third of the fire bed and 1 or 2 layers deep in another third of the fire bed, leaving the remaining third free of coals. Replace the grill grate in its slots. **IF YOU ARE USING A GAS GRILL,** turn on all of the heat elements as high as they will go. **FOR EITHER TYPE OF GRILL,** place serving plates near the grill to warm from its heat, or warm them in a 200°F (95°C) oven. Scrub the grill grate with a wire brush to remove any traces of food. Then, lightly rub the grill grate with paper towels coated with canola oil. For more details on oiling the grill grate, turn to page 39. ❯

For the lime-beer marinade

2 cloves garlic, peeled

⅓ cup (½ oz/15 g) packed fresh cilantro (fresh coriander) leaves

½ cup (4 fl oz/125 ml) lager-style beer, preferably Mexican

Grated zest of 1 lime (page 36)

¼ cup (2 fl oz/60 ml) fresh lime juice (page 36)

¼ cup (2 fl oz/60 ml) extra-virgin olive oil

1 tablespoon chili powder

1 teaspoon ground cumin

1 teaspoon dried oregano

¼ teaspoon ground chipotle chile or cayenne pepper, optional

½ teaspoon salt

1 flank steak, about 1¾ lb (875 g)

Canola oil for coating the grill grate

MAKES 4 SERVINGS

CHEF'S TIP

Skirt steak can also be used for making carne asada. It is a relatively long, flat cut and, like flank steak, has enormous flavor. Also like flank steak, though fairly lean, it has just enough fat to keep it juicy over the high heat of the grill.

4 Grill the steak

Before grilling, test the grill temperature. **IF YOU ARE USING A CHARCOAL GRILL,** hold your hand about 4 inches (10 cm) above the fire. If you can count only to 1 before pulling your hand away (very high heat), the coals are ready. **IF YOU ARE USING A GAS GRILL,** leave all of the heat elements on high. The temperature should reach 500°F (260°C) before you begin to cook. **FOR EITHER TYPE OF GRILL,** when the grill is ready, remove the steak from the marinade and let the excess marinade drip off. Discard the marinade. Place the steak over the hottest area of the grill, and cover, if desired (see page 9). Grill the steak until the underside is browned (the moisture from the marinade prevents a dark brown surface crust from forming), about 4 minutes. If you want cross-hatching on the steak, use long-handled tongs to rotate it 90 degrees after 2 minutes of cooking. If you need help creating cross-hatching, turn to page 41. Use the tongs to turn over the steak and grill until the second side is browned, about 4 minutes more for medium-rare, again rotating the steak 90 degrees if cross-hatching is desired.

5 Check the steak for doneness

Insert an instant-read thermometer horizontally into the center of the steak, or, if necessary, cut into it near the center. At medium-rare, the thermometer should read 140°F (60°C) or the color should be deep pink. If the steak is not ready, cover the grill, let it cook for 1–2 minutes longer, and test again. To find out more about checking meat for doneness, turn to page 42.

6 Let the steak rest

When the steak is done to your liking, transfer it to a carving board and let it rest for 3–5 minutes. This brief rest before serving allows the juices to redistribute throughout the meat. The temperature of the steak will also rise about 5°F (3°C) while resting. If cut too soon, the steak will not have its optimal juiciness and the color inside will be uneven.

7 Clean and maintain the grill for the next use

While the meat is resting, use a sturdy grill brush to clean the still-hot grill. **IF YOU ARE USING A CHARCOAL GRILL,** cover it and let the coals burn out completely. **IF YOU ARE USING A GAS GRILL,** turn off the heat elements, seal the propane tank, and close the grill cover.

8 Slice the steak and serve

Turn the steak on the carving board so that the long end is facing you and the direction of the muscle fibers runs horizontally. The fibers are referred to as the meat's *grain*, because they resemble the grain in a plank of wood. Use a meat fork to hold the steak steady. In the other hand, hold a thin-bladed carving knife perpendicular to the steak at a 45-degree angle, and cut the steak across the grain into thin slices about ¼ inch (6 mm) thick. This shortens the long, tough muscle fibers and makes the meat easier to chew. Transfer the sliced steak to the warmed plates. Pour any juices from the board over the slices and serve right away.

Carne Asada Variations

Marinating a lean cut to impart moisture, grilling to no more than medium-rare, and slicing against the grain to ensure tenderness are just three keys to making successful Carne Asada (page 59). Now that you have practiced these skills on a Latin American favorite, you are ready to apply them to other internationally inspired beef dishes, including these three variations—with *salsa verde, chimichurri,* and teriyaki—all of which double here as both marinades and table sauces. In all three cases, set aside half of the marinade for the sauce before you begin marinating, to avoid possible bacterial contamination from uncooked meat. Each variation makes 4 servings.

Steak with Salsa Verde

Salsa verde, a green Italian sauce, is usually served as a condiment for meats, but it makes a delicious marinade, too.

In a food processor, combine 2 cups (3 oz/90 g) packed fresh flat-leaf (Italian) parsley leaves, ¼ cup (2 oz/60 g) rinsed and drained capers, and 2 chopped garlic cloves; pulse until finely chopped. In a bowl, whisk together ¼ cup (2 fl oz/60 ml) red wine vinegar, 2 teaspoons anchovy paste, 2 teaspoons Dijon mustard, and ¼ teaspoon red pepper flakes. Whisk in ¾ cup (6 fl oz/180 ml) extra-virgin olive oil. Stir in the parsley mixture. Pour ¾ cup (6 fl oz/180 ml) into a serving bowl, cover, and refrigerate.

Put 1 flank steak, about 1¾ lb (875 g), in a shallow ceramic or glass dish. Add the remaining parsley mixture, cover, and refrigerate for 4–24 hours. Remove from the refrigerator 1 hour before grilling.

Prepare a charcoal or gas grill for direct grilling over very high heat. Oil the grill grate. Remove the steak from the marinade and grill, turning once, until done to your liking, about 4 minutes per side for medium-rare. Let rest for 3–5 minutes. Thinly slice across the grain. Serve right away, with the sauce.

Steak with Chimichurri

In Argentina, this intense parsley-based sauce is offered alongside steak. In this recipe, it also acts as a marinade.

In a food processor, combine 1½ cups (3 oz/90 g) packed fresh flat-leaf (Italian) parsley leaves, ½ coarsely chopped small yellow onion, and 2 chopped garlic cloves; pulse until finely chopped. In a bowl, whisk together ¼ cup (2 fl oz/60 ml) red wine vinegar, 1½ teaspoons dried oregano, ½ teaspoon salt, and ¾ teaspoon red pepper flakes. Whisk in 1 cup (8 fl oz/250 ml) extra-virgin olive oil. Stir in the garlic mixture. Pour ½ cup (4 fl oz/125 ml) of the mixture into a serving bowl, cover, and refrigerate.

Put 1 flank steak, about 1¾ lb (875 g), in a shallow ceramic or glass dish. Add the remaining parsley mixture, cover, and refrigerate for 4–24 hours. Remove from the refrigerator 1 hour before grilling.

Prepare a charcoal or gas grill for direct grilling over very high heat. Oil the grill grate. Remove the steak from the marinade and grill, turning once, until done to your liking, about 4 minutes per side for medium-rare. Let rest for 3–5 minutes. Thinly slice across the grain. Serve right away, with the sauce.

Teriyaki-Style Steak

Teriyaki owes its sweetness to mirin, a cooking wine, and brown sugar.

In a bowl, whisk 1 cup (8 fl oz/250 ml) soy sauce; ¼ cup (2 fl oz/60 ml) *each* sake, mirin, and Asian sesame oil; ¼ cup (2 fl oz/60 ml) firmly packed golden brown sugar; ½ teaspoon red pepper flakes; 6 thin slices fresh ginger; 4 crushed garlic cloves; and 2 thinly sliced green (spring) onions. Pour ½ cup (4 fl oz/125 ml) into a bowl, cover, and refrigerate.

Put 1 flank steak, about 1¾ lb (875 g), in a shallow ceramic or glass dish. Add the remaining marinade, cover, and refrigerate for 4–24 hours. Remove from the refrigerator 1 hour before grilling.

Prepare a charcoal or gas grill for direct grilling over very high heat. Oil the grill grate. Remove the steak from the marinade, reserving the marinade, and grill, turning once, until done to your liking, about 4 minutes per side for medium-rare. Let the steak rest for 3–5 minutes. Strain the marinade into a saucepan, bring to a boil, whisk in 1 teaspoon cornstarch (cornflour) dissolved in 2 tablespoons water, and cook until thickened. Thinly slice the steak across the grain. Serve right away, with the sauce.

Pork Satay with Peanut Sauce

Satay, skewered meat, is a popular street food in Southeast Asia, where smoky charcoal fires give the small kebabs a wonderful flavor. Here, pork loin, a lean, tender cut, is treated to a sweet-hot-spicy marinade before grilling, and the skewers are served with a rich peanut sauce, laced with ginger and pepper flakes, for dipping.

For the peanut sauce

1 tablespoon canola oil

3 tablespoons finely diced shallots (page 32)

3 slices fresh ginger, each ¼ inch (6 mm) thick, finely chopped (about 1 tablespoon) (page 35)

2 cloves garlic, minced (page 33)

1 teaspoon curry powder

⅛ teaspoon red pepper flakes

1¼ cups (10 fl oz/310 ml) Brown Poultry Stock (page 24) or low-sodium chicken broth

½ cup (5 oz/155 g) chunky-style peanut butter

1 tablespoon fresh lime juice (page 36)

1 tablespoon soy sauce

1 teaspoon firmly packed golden brown sugar

1½ lb (750 g) center-cut boneless pork loin roast

For the marinade

¼ cup (2 fl oz/60 ml) soy sauce

Grated zest of 2 limes (page 36)

2 tablespoons fresh lime juice (page 36)

2 tablespoons canola oil

1 tablespoon curry powder

1 tablespoon firmly packed golden brown sugar

2 cloves garlic, finely chopped (page 33)

Canola oil for coating the grill grate

1 bunch fresh chives, optional

1 tablespoon chopped peanuts

MAKES 4 MAIN-COURSE OR
6–8 APPETIZER SERVINGS

1 **Make the peanut sauce**
In a heavy-bottomed saucepan, heat the oil over medium heat. When the oil appears to shimmer, add the shallots and cook uncovered, stirring often, until the shallots soften, about 2 minutes. Add the ginger and garlic and stir until fragrant, about 1 minute. Stir in the curry powder and red pepper flakes and cook just to heat the curry powder, about 15 seconds. Add the stock, peanut butter, lime juice, soy sauce, and brown sugar. Whisking often, heat until small bubbles begin to form on the surface of the sauce; this is a *simmer.* Reduce the heat to medium-low and simmer, stirring often, to blend the flavors, about 3 minutes. Remove from the heat. (The sauce can be kept at room temperature, covered, for up to 2 hours. To store longer, transfer the cooled sauce to a bowl, cover, and refrigerate for up to 2 days.)

2 **Soak the skewers**
Bamboo skewers will burn from the heat of the grill if not soaked before use. Place 32 bamboo skewers each 6 inches (15 cm) long, in a shallow dish just large enough to hold them, and cover with cold water. Let stand for 30 minutes–2 hours; if you soak them for longer than 2 hours, they could become too soft.

3 **Cut the pork into strips**
Put the pork on a cutting board. Using a boning knife or chef's knife, trim away the surface fat from the pork. For more details on trimming roasts, turn to page 37. Cut the pork loin crosswise into slices ½ inch (12 mm) thick. Place each slice on the board, and cut the slices into strips ½ inch (12 mm) thick. You will need 32 pork strips for this recipe; reserve any extras for another use.

4 **Make the marinade**
In a bowl, whisk together the soy sauce, lime zest and juice, oil, curry powder, brown sugar, and garlic until the sugar is dissolved.

5 **Marinate the pork**
Put the pork strips and marinade in a shallow ceramic or glass dish just large enough to hold the pork. Do not use metal, which may react with the acids in the marinade and impart off flavors. Cover the dish tightly with plastic wrap. (Alternatively, marinate the pork in a locking plastic bag.) Refrigerate the pork and marinade for at least 30 minutes or up to 2 hours, turning the meat occasionally. Remove the pork in its marinade from the refrigerator 30 minutes before grilling.

6 Prepare the grill

If you need help setting up a grill, turn to pages 38–39. About 20 minutes before you start cooking, prepare a charcoal or gas grill with 2 areas of high heat and 1 cooler area: **IF YOU ARE USING A CHARCOAL GRILL,** first remove the grill grate and set it aside. Next, ignite the briquettes and/or charcoal using a chimney starter and let them burn until they are covered with white ash. Then, pour the coals into the fire bed. Finally, using long-handled tongs, spread the hot coals 2 or 3 layers deep in one-third of the fire bed and 1 or 2 layers deep in another third of the fire bed, leaving the remaining third free of coals. Replace the grill grate in its slots. **IF YOU ARE USING A GAS GRILL,** turn on all of the heat elements as high as they will go. **FOR EITHER TYPE OF GRILL,** place a serving platter or serving plates near the grill to warm from its heat, or warm it in a 200°F (95°C) oven. You will use the platter or plates to serve the skewers and sauce. Scrub the grill grate with a wire brush to remove any traces of food. Then, lightly rub the grill grate with paper towels coated with canola oil; for more details on oiling the grill grate, turn to page 39.

7 Skewer the pork

While the grill is heating, drain the skewers. Remove the pork strips from the marinade, then weave them, accordion style, onto the skewers. This will secure the meat and keep it from spinning on the skewer when it is turned, and it will give the pork a nice presentation. Try to cover the tip of the skewer with meat. If you wish to protect the skewers further from scorching, wrap the bare "handle" ends of the skewer with small pieces of aluminum foil.

8 Grill the satay

Before grilling, test the grill temperature. **IF YOU ARE USING A CHARCOAL GRILL,** hold your hand about 4 inches (10 cm) above the fire. If you can count to 1 or 2 seconds before pulling your hand away (high heat), the coals are ready. **IF YOU ARE USING A GAS GRILL,** leave 1 or 2 heat elements on high and turn the other heat element on low. The temperature should reach 425°F (220°C) before you begin to cook. **FOR EITHER TYPE OF GRILL,** when the grill is ready, place the skewers over the hottest part of the grill and cover, if desired (see page 9). Grill the pork, turning once or twice, until lightly marked by the grill and slightly pink on the inside when pierced with the tip of a small knife, about 6 minutes total. Do not overcook the pork or it will be dry. If the dripping juices cause flare-ups, move the skewers to the cooler part of the grill, where the juices are less likely to ignite, and continue to cook. If desired, line the platter with fresh chives for an unusual but eye-catching garnish. When the pork is done, transfer the skewers to the warmed platter. Remove the aluminum foil if you covered the skewer ends. (Remember to clean the grill while it is still hot.)

9 Reheat the sauce and serve the satay

Reheat the sauce over low heat. If the sauce has thickened, whisk in more stock, 1 tablespoon at a time, until it is smooth. Transfer to a serving bowl and sprinkle with the chopped peanuts. Serve the skewers right away with sauce.

Satay Variations

Nearly every cuisine has its own version of marinated and skewered meat or poultry (and seafood, too), sometimes served with a savory dipping sauce. In Pork Satay with Peanut Sauce (page 62), you learned a variety of key skills—how to soak bamboo skewers to keep them from burning on the grill, how to skewer meat, how to grill meat to its optimal flavor and tenderness—that you can now use to prepare other skewered meat. Here are three delicious options, Japanese-style beef, Middle Eastern–style lamb, and Caribbean-style chicken. All are seasoned differently, but all are grilled in essentially the same way. Each variation makes 4 main-course or 6–8 appetizer servings.

Sake-Ginger Beef Skewers

This marinade is similar to teriyaki but not as sweet. A sake dipping sauce provides another layer of flavor.

Soak 32 bamboo skewers, 6 inches (15 cm) long, in water for 30 minutes, then drain. Trim the fat from 2 rib-eye steaks, each about ¾ lb (375 g) and ½ inch (12 mm) thick. Cut the meat at a 45-degree angle into strips about ¼ inch (6 mm) wide.

In a bowl, whisk together ¾ cup (6 fl oz/180 ml) soy sauce, 3 tablespoons sake, 3 tablespoons firmly packed golden brown sugar, 3 tablespoons Asian sesame oil, 2 teaspoons minced fresh ginger, 3 crushed garlic cloves, ½ teaspoon red pepper flakes, and 1 thinly sliced green (spring) onion (white and pale green parts). Put the beef and marinade in a shallow ceramic or glass dish. Cover and marinate for 30 minutes.

In a bowl, whisk ¾ cup (6 fl oz/180 ml) sake, 2 tablespoons rice vinegar, and 1 teaspoon minced fresh ginger.

Prepare a charcoal or gas grill for direct grilling over high heat. Oil the grill grate. Weave the beef strips onto the skewers. Grill the meat, turning, until done to your liking, about 4 minutes total for medium-rare. Serve right away with the sake-ginger dipping sauce.

Lamb Kebabs with Mint-Yogurt Marinade

Yogurt may seem an unlikely marinade for lamb, but it chars lightly on the grill to leave a great-tasting exterior.

Soak 16 bamboo skewers, 6 inches (15 cm) long, in water to cover for 30 minutes, then drain. Trim the surface fat and sinew from 3 lb (1.5 kg) boneless leg of lamb. Cut the lamb into 1½-inch (4-cm) squares. (After trimming, you will end up with about 1½ lb/750 g lamb.)

In a bowl, stir together 1 cup (8 oz/250 g) plain low-fat yogurt, 3 tablespoons finely chopped fresh mint, 2 finely chopped garlic cloves, 1 teaspoon ground cumin, ½ teaspoon salt, and ¼ teaspoon red pepper flakes. Put the lamb and marinade in a shallow ceramic or glass dish. Cover and marinate for 30 minutes.

Prepare a charcoal or gas grill for direct grilling over high heat. Oil the grill grate. Thread 2 chunks of lamb into each skewer, leaving space between the chunks. Grill the lamb until it is lightly browned on all sides, about 2 minutes per side for medium-rare. Serve right away.

Jerk Chicken Skewers

A Jamaican marinade will add bold flavor to chicken. Try it with pork, too, using the directions for the satay.

Soak 32 bamboo skewers, 6 inches (15 cm) long, in water to cover for 30 minutes, then drain. Trim the surface fat from 2 lb (1 kg) boneless, skinless chicken breast halves. Cut the chicken crosswise at a 45-degree angle into strips ½-inch (12-mm) wide. Lightly pound the strips to be about ¼ inch (6 mm) thick and 3 inches (7.5 cm) wide.

In a food processor, combine 6 chopped green (spring) onions (white and pale green parts), ½ seeded, deribbed, and minced Scotch bonnet chile, 4 minced garlic cloves, ¼ cup (2 fl oz/60 ml) canola oil, ¼ cup (2 fl oz/60 ml) fresh lime juice, 2 tablespoons soy sauce, 2 teaspoons dried thyme, and 1 teaspoon ground allspice. Put the chicken strips and the marinade in a shallow ceramic or glass dish. Cover and marinate for 30 minutes.

Prepare a charcoal or gas grill for direct grilling over high heat. Oil the grill grate. Weave the chicken strips onto the skewers. Grill the chicken, turning, until opaque throughout, about 6 minutes total; the meat should not be pink. Serve right away.

Chicken under a Brick

In this Italian method for cooking chicken, the bird is opened flat and then marinated in a piquant lemon mixture redolent with garlic. The trick of grilling the chicken under a heavy weight (traditionally a brick) exposes the maximum amount of the bird to the heat, resulting in golden, crisp skin and moist flesh.

1 Remove the backbone
Place the chicken, breast side down, on a cutting board. Using kitchen scissors, cut along one side of the backbone from the tail end to the neck end. (You can also use a large chef's knife for this step: place the knife just to the right or left of the backbone and use firm pressure to make a clean cut.) Pull open the halves of the chicken, taking care not to rip or tear the skin. Cut down along the other side of the backbone to free it. Discard the backbone or save it for stock.

2 Flatten the chicken
Turn the chicken breast side up, opening the cavity so that it is lying as flat as possible. Placing one hand over the other, press firmly on the breast area to break the breastbone and completely flatten the bird. (If you do not hear and feel the bone crack, repeat this process until the bone is broken.)

3 Secure the wings
Working with one side of the bird at a time, tuck each wing akimbo, securing the tip end behind each shoulder. This technique of removing the backbone and leaving the bird flat, called *butterflying,* will leave the bird with two wide sides connected by a thinner central area. It will somewhat resemble a butterfly.

4 Chop the garlic, and zest and juice the lemon
Place the garlic cloves on the cutting board, firmly press against them with the flat side of a chef's knife, and pull away and discard the papery skins. Rock the knife blade back and forth and up and down to chop the garlic. If you are not sure how to chop garlic, turn to page 33. Using a rasp grater, such as a fine Microplane grater, grate the colored part of the lemon peel until you have 2 teaspoons grated zest. Next, cut the lemon in half and use a reamer to extract ⅓ cup (3 fl oz/80 ml) juice. For more details on zesting and juicing citrus fruit, turn to page 36.

1 large chicken, about 4 lb (2 kg), neck and giblets removed

3 cloves garlic

1 lemon

2 tablespoons extra-virgin olive oil

1 teaspoon dried oregano

¾ teaspoon salt

¾ teaspoon red pepper flakes

Canola oil for coating the grill grate

Lemon wedges for serving

MAKES 4 SERVINGS

CHEF'S TIP
Using oil as the marinade base will prevent the chicken from sticking to the grill. But be careful about how much you use. An excess can cause flare-ups.

5>

5 Marinate the chicken

In a bowl, whisk together the garlic, lemon zest and juice, olive oil, oregano, salt, and red pepper flakes until well blended. Put the chicken and marinade in a shallow ceramic or glass dish. Cover tightly and refrigerate for at least 30 minutes or up to 2 hours. Remove from the refrigerator 30 minutes before grilling.

6 Prepare the grill

If you need help setting up a grill, turn to pages 38–39. About 20 minutes before you start cooking, prepare a charcoal or gas grill with 1 area of high heat and 1 cooler area: **IF YOU ARE USING A CHARCOAL GRILL,** first remove the grill grate and set it aside. Next, ignite the briquettes and/or charcoal using a chimney starter and let them burn until they are covered with white ash. Then, pour the coals into the fire bed. Using long-handled tongs, spread the hot coals 2 or 3 layers deep in one-half of the fire bed and just 1 layer deep in the other half. Replace the grill grate. **IF YOU ARE USING A GAS GRILL,** turn on all of the heat elements as high as they will go. **FOR EITHER TYPE OF GRILL,** place serving plates near the grill to warm from its heat, or warm them in a 200°F (95°C) oven. Scrub the grill grate with a wire brush to remove any traces of food. Then, lightly rub the grate with paper towels coated with canola oil; for more details, turn to page 39. You'll also need 1 heavy cast-iron skillet or 2 bricks wrapped in aluminum foil to weight down the chicken.

7 Grill the chicken

Before grilling, test the grill temperature. **IF YOU ARE USING A CHARCOAL GRILL,** hold your hand about 4 inches (10 cm) above the fire. If you can count to 1 or 2 seconds before pulling your hand away (high heat), the coals are ready. **IF YOU ARE USING A GAS GRILL,** leave 1 or 2 heat elements on high and turn the other heat element to low. The temperature should reach 425°F (220°C) before you begin to cook. **FOR EITHER TYPE OF GRILL,** remove the chicken from the marinade and place, skin side down, over the low-heat part of the grill. Discard the marinade. Place the skillet or bricks on top of the chicken, cover the grill, and cook until the skin is golden brown, about 30 minutes. >

CHEF'S TIP
When you are working with a marinade that has an acidic component, such as lemon juice, always pay close attention to the marinating time. If the meat sits too long in the marinade, its flavor and color can change.

8 Turn over the chicken

If the dripping juices cause flare-ups, move the chicken to the edge of a charcoal grill or turn off the heat element on a gas grill and continue to cook. This way, the drippings will be less likely to ignite. Turn over the chicken, replace the skillet or bricks, and cover the grill. Cook for about 15 minutes longer.

9 Check the chicken for doneness

Remove the pan or bricks. Insert an instant-read thermometer into the thickest part of the breast, not touching a bone. It should read 170°F (77°C). If the chicken is not done, replace the skillet or bricks, cook for another 5 minutes, and then test again. If you are not sure how to test poultry for doneness, turn to page 43.

CHEF'S TIP

If you don't have a thermometer, transfer the chicken to a white plate or platter and pierce the thigh joint with the tip of a paring knife. The juices (which will be easy to gauge against the white surface) should run clear yellow. Any trace of pink or red in the juices indicates that the chicken must cook longer.

10 Let the chicken rest

Transfer the chicken to a carving board (a cutting board with a groove around the outside to capture the juices) and let it rest for 5 minutes. This allows the juices to redistribute throughout the chicken. The temperature of the chicken will also rise 5°–10°F (3°–6°C).

11 Clean and maintain the grill for the next use

While the chicken is resting, use a sturdy grill brush to clean the still-hot grill grate. **IF YOU ARE USING A CHARCOAL GRILL,** cover it and let the coals burn out completely. **IF YOU ARE USING A GAS GRILL,** turn off the heat elements, seal the propane tank, and close the grill cover.

12 Quarter and serve the chicken

Position the breastbone facing away from you. Using a chef's knife, and firm pressure, cut the chicken in half lengthwise through the breastbone. Then, cut each portion in half where the breast area meets the thigh. Transfer the breasts and thigh-leg portions to the warmed plates. Serve right away with lemon wedges.

Serving ideas

When cooking main courses on the grill, it is always helpful to consider cooking your side dishes on the grill as well. You will need to plan carefully to ensure that the timing and heat level for the main and sides are compatible. Tomato halves will cook fast on the hottest part of the grill, and grilled peaches cook just as quickly. Potato wedges, however, take longer, and they also require parboiling. Be sure to plan ahead.

Chicken with grilled tomatoes (top left)
While the chicken rests, put 4 tomato halves on the hottest part of the grill for about 2½ minutes per side, or until the skin is blistered. Season with salt, pepper, and chopped fresh oregano.

Chicken with grilled peaches (left)
While the chicken rests, follow the instructions on page 130 for grilling peaches. Serve them on a platter with the quartered chicken.

Chicken with grilled potato wedges (above)
Cut 3 or 4 russet potatoes into wedges. Parboil the potatoes (page 129). When you turn the chicken in step 8, place the potatoes on the cooler part of the grill and cook, turning occasionally, for 15 minutes.

Grilled Tuna with Red Pepper Relish

Fresh, thick tuna steaks, with their distinctively meaty quality, are a good match for the subtly smoky, mildly spicy chunky red pepper condiment that accompanies them. The fish steaks are seared over high heat, which contributes flavor and color, while the interior is left medium-rare to rare for a tender, sea-fresh fish taste.

For the red pepper relish

12 large sprigs fresh oregano

3 tablespoons pine nuts

1 green (spring) onion

3 red bell peppers (capsicums), about 1½ lb (1.25 kg) total weight

1 tablespoon balsamic vinegar

1 tablespoon honey

1 tablespoon extra-virgin olive oil

¼ teaspoon salt

¼ teaspoon red pepper flakes

4 tuna steaks, each 6 oz (185 g) and about 1 inch (2.5 cm) thick

2 tablespoons extra-virgin olive oil

½ teaspoon salt

½ teaspoon freshly ground pepper

Canola oil for coating the grill grate

MAKES 4 SERVINGS

CHEF'S TIP

Any type of tuna can be used for this recipe. The most popular types include albacore, yellowfin or ahi, and bluefin. Look for sashimi-grade tuna if you like to cook and serve the tuna rare.

1 Prepare the grill

If you need help setting up a grill, turn to pages 38–39. About 20 minutes before you start cooking, prepare a charcoal or gas grill with 2 areas of high heat and 1 cooler area.

2 Prepare the ingredients for the relish

Pull the leaves off the stems of the oregano sprigs, discard the stems, and pile the leaves on a cutting board. Using a chef's knife, finely chop the oregano: Hold the knife tip with one hand so it stays on the board, then rock the heel of the knife over the leaves to cut them into small pieces; you should have about 2 tablespoons. If you are not sure how to chop herbs, turn to page 35. Next, toast the pine nuts: Heat a small, dry frying pan over high heat until the pan is hot. Add the pine nuts and heat, stirring frequently, until the nuts are toasted, 3–5 minutes. Transfer the nuts to a plate and let cool. For more information on toasting nuts, turn to page 36. Finally, trim the green onions, line them up on the cutting board, and thinly slice crosswise, including the pale green parts. For more details on working with green onions, turn to page 34.

3 Prepare the peppers

Working with 1 bell pepper at a time, and using a chef's knife, cut a slice ½ inch (12 mm) thick off the top and bottom. Cut out and discard the stem; reserve the top and bottom. Make a lengthwise cut down one side of the pepper and open the pepper so that it lies flat, skin side down, on the cutting board. Cut out the white ribs and seeds and discard.

4 Grill the peppers

IF YOU ARE USING A CHARCOAL GRILL, hold your hand about 4 inches (10 cm) above the fire. If you can count only to 1 before pulling your hand away (very high heat), the coals are ready. **IF YOU ARE USING A GAS GRILL,** the temperature should reach 500°F (260°C) before you begin to cook. **FOR EITHER TYPE OF GRILL,** place the peppers, including tops and bottoms, over the hottest part of the grill, shiny skin sides down (when grilling peppers, there is no need to oil the grill grate or the peppers because the natural oils in the peppers work as a lubricant). Cover the grill, if desired (see page 9). Grill until the pepper skins are blistered and blackened, about 8 minutes (if some areas remain unblackened, that's fine). Use tongs to transfer the blackened peppers to a bowl. Let the peppers cool until they are easy to handle, about 10 minutes. ›

5 Peel the peppers and make the relish

Peel off and discard the blackened skin from the peppers. You can use a paring knife to scrape away or trim off any stubborn patches. Do not rinse the peppers. Chop the peppers into ½-inch (12-mm) pieces. In a bowl, whisk together the vinegar, honey, olive oil, salt, and red pepper flakes until the honey is dissolved. Add the oregano, pine nuts, diced red bell pepper, and green onion, and mix well with a wooden spoon. Transfer to a serving bowl and cover. Let stand at room temperature to blend the flavors while you are cooking the tuna.

6 Grill the tuna

About 10 minutes before you plan to eat, test the grill temperature: **IF YOU ARE USING A CHARCOAL GRILL,** and you can count only to 1 before pulling your hand away (very high heat), the coals are ready. If it is too cool (you can keep your hand over the fire for more than 3 seconds), add more coals to the fire bed and let burn until the coals are medium-hot again. Replace the grill grate in its slots. **IF YOU ARE USING A GAS GRILL,** the temperature should reach 500°F (260°C) before you begin to cook. **FOR EITHER TYPE OF GRILL,** place serving plates near the grill to warm from its heat, or warm them in a 200°F (95°C) oven. Brush the tuna steaks lightly on both sides with the olive oil. Season on both sides with the salt and pepper. Then, lightly rub the grill grate with paper towels coated with canola oil. For more information on oiling the grill grate, turn to page 39. Place the tuna steaks over the hottest part of the fire. Grill, turning once with a long-handled spatula, until they are seared on the outside and rare to medium-rare on the inside, 3–5 minutes per side. If you want cross-hatching on your fish, use the spatula to rotate the steaks 90 degrees after 1½–2½ minutes of cooking on each side. For more details on cross-hatching, turn to page 41.

7 Test the tuna for doneness

Use a paring knife to cut into the tuna near the center. For rare tuna, it should be very red in the middle, with a ring of brownish flesh around the outside. If you like your tuna medium-rare, the middle will be dark pink. For more information on testing fish for doneness, turn to page 43. Transfer the tuna steaks to a cutting board and let stand for 3 minutes to ease slicing.

8 Maintain the grill for the next use

While the tuna is resting, use a sturdy grill brush to clean the still-hot grill grate.

9 Serve the tuna and relish

Using a chef's knife, slice the tuna across the grain and transfer to warmed dinner plates, fanning out the slices. Serve right away, with a large spoonful of the relish next to the fish. Pass any remaining relish at the table.

Grilled Fish with Vegetable Relish Variations

When you are choosing fish for the grill, avoid thin fillets, which tend to fall apart when you turn them. Meaty fish steaks and fillets are both candidates, as you learned in Grilled Tuna with Red Pepper Relish (page 72). The techniques you now know, oiling the steaks or fillets lightly and using a medium-high fire, can be used for other kinds of fish, all of which are delicious when accompanied with a colorful vegetable or fruit relish or salsa. Here are three interesting combinations: salmon with pineapple, mahimahi with mango, and swordfish with tomatoes and olives. Each variation makes 4 servings.

Salmon with Pineapple Salsa

Choose a ripe pineapple for this sweet and spicy salsa.

Prepare a charcoal or gas grill for direct grilling over high heat. Oil the grill grate.

Cut ½ peeled and cored pineapple into slices ½ inch (12 mm) thick. Grill, turning once, until lightly marked by the grill, about 4 minutes total. Transfer the pineapple to a cutting board, cut into ½-inch (12-mm) dice, and put the dice in a bowl. Add ¼ cup (2 oz/60 g) finely chopped red bell pepper (capsicum); 2 tablespoons chopped fresh cilantro (fresh coriander); the grated zest of 1 lime; 2 tablespoons fresh lime juice; 1 finely chopped green (spring) onion (white and pale green parts); 1 seeded, deribbed, and minced jalapeño; and ¼ teaspoon salt. Mix gently, then cover and set aside.

Brush 4 salmon steaks, 7–8 oz (220–250 g) each and about ½ inch (12 mm) thick, with 2 tablespoons extra-virgin olive oil. Season with ½ teaspoon salt and ¼ teaspoon pepper. Grill, turning once, until opaque throughout, about 8 minutes total. Serve right away with a spoonful of the salsa.

Mahimahi with Mango Salsa

Grilled snapper and grouper are also good with this salsa.

Prepare a charcoal or gas grill for direct grilling over high heat. Oil the grill grate.

Halve 3 ripe mangoes, cutting down both sides of each fruit about 1 inch (2.5 cm) from the stem to avoid the pit. Discard the pit and peel the halves. Grill the mango halves, turning once, until the halves are lightly marked by the grill, about 4 minutes total. Transfer the mangoes to a cutting board, cut into ½-inch (12-mm) dice, and transfer to a bowl. Add ½ seeded, deribbed, and minced Scotch bonnet chile, 1 teaspoon finely chopped fresh ginger, 2 tablespoons finely chopped fresh cilantro (fresh coriander), 2 tablespoons rice vinegar, and a pinch of salt. Mix gently, cover, and set aside.

Brush 4 mahimahi fillets, about 6 oz (185 g) each, with 2 tablespoons extra-virgin olive oil. Season with ½ teaspoon salt and ¼ teaspoon pepper. Grill, turning once, until opaque throughout, 6–8 minutes total. Serve right away with a spoonful of salsa.

Swordfish with Tomato-Olive Relish

A signature Mediterranean dish pairs this Italian relish of grilled tomatoes and olives with fresh-caught swordfish.

Prepare a charcoal or gas grill for direct grilling over high heat. Oil the grill grate.

Grill 5 plum (Roma) tomatoes until the skins are charred on all sides, about 7 minutes total. Transfer to a bowl. When cool enough to handle, use a paring knife to peel off the tomato skins. Cut each tomato in half crosswise. Scoop out the seeds. Coarsely chop the tomatoes and transfer to a bowl. Add ⅓ cup (2 oz/60 g) chopped Mediterranean-style black olives, 2 tablespoons chopped fresh basil, 1 tablespoon red wine vinegar, 1 tablespoon extra-virgin olive oil, 1 minced garlic clove, ¼ teaspoon salt, and ⅛ teaspoon red pepper flakes and mix well. Cover for at least 20 minutes.

Brush 4 swordfish fillets, 7–8 oz (220–250 g) each, with 2 tablespoons extra-virgin olive oil. Season with ½ teaspoon salt and ¼ teaspoon pepper. Grill, turning once, until opaque throughout, 6–8 minutes total. Serve right away with a spoonful of relish.

Grill-Roasted Trout with Mint, Lemon & Pecan Stuffing

Filled with a hearty bread crumb, mint, and pecan stuffing, these small fish make a light yet satisfying main course. They are cooked in a hinged basket, which makes them easy to turn on the grill. The skin turns a light brown over the fire, while the stuffing heats through, melding the flavors.

1 **Soak the bamboo skewers, if needed**
You'll need 4 bamboo or thin metal skewers for this recipe. If you are using bamboo skewers, soak them in water to cover for at least 30 minutes.

2 **Make the stuffing and stuff the trout**
Cut the crust from the bread, tear the slices into large pieces, and place in a food processor. Process until coarse crumbs form. Measure out 2 cups (4 oz/125 g) and reserve the remainder for another use. Pour the crumbs into a bowl. Add the pecans, mint, melted butter, lemon zest, salt, and pepper and mix well. Taste for seasoning, keeping in mind the fish will be seasoned as well.

3 **Stuff the trout**
Pat the trout dry with paper towels and stuff the cavities with equal amounts of the filling. Weave a soaked bamboo or metal skewer, accordion style, through each fish to secure the body cavity closed. Brush the fish on both sides with the oil, then sprinkle with the salt and pepper. Loosely cover with plastic wrap and refrigerate while preparing the grill.

4 **Prepare the grill and grill baskets**
If you need help setting up a grill, turn to pages 38–39. About 20 minutes before you start cooking, prepare a charcoal or gas grill for direct grilling over medium heat. Oil the inside of 1 large or 2 small hinged grilling baskets.

5 **Grill the trout and serve**
Before grilling, test the grill temperature: **IF YOU ARE USING A CHARCOAL GRILL,** hold your hand about 4 inches (10 cm) above the fire. If you can count to 2 or 3 seconds before pulling your hand away (medium-high heat), the coals are ready. **IF YOU ARE USING A GAS GRILL,** the temperature should reach 375°F (190°C) before you begin to cook. **FOR EITHER TYPE OF GRILL,** arrange the fish in a single layer in the grill basket(s) and place on the grill. Grill, turning once, until the fish are lightly browned and the flesh looks opaque when pierced with a pairing knife, 8–10 minutes total. Transfer the fish to warmed plates and serve right away with lemon wedges. Instruct the diners to remove the skewers and to watch for any small bones in the fish. (Remember to clean the grill while it is still hot.)

For the mint and pecan stuffing

4 large slices day-old coarse Italian bread

½ cup (2 oz/60 g) pecan halves, toasted (page 36) and coarsely chopped

¼ cup (½ oz/15 g) chopped fresh mint (page 35)

4 tablespoons unsalted butter, melted

Grated zest of 1 lemon

¼ teaspoon salt

⅛ teaspoon freshly ground pepper

4 rainbow trout, about ¾ lb (375 g) each, cleaned and rinsed with the head and tail intact

Canola oil for brushing the fish

1 teaspoon salt

½ teaspoon freshly ground pepper

Lemon wedges for serving

MAKES 4 SERVINGS

 CHEF'S TIP
Dried bread crumbs and fresh bread crumbs are not interchangeable, as fresh crumbs have more moisture than dried crumbs and the two will behave differently in recipes.

Grill-Roasted Mussels with White Wine & Shallots

Mussels cooked with wine, herbs, and garlic are traditionally prepared on a stove top, but there's no reason why they can't be grilled in a cast-iron frying pan. In fact, they will pick up a delicate smokiness that may make this version a favorite. Accompany them with lots of crusty bread to soak up the aromatic cooking liquid.

2 shallots

1 clove garlic

½ bunch fresh flat-leaf (Italian) parsley

2 lb (1 kg) natural or farm-raised mussels

2 tablespoons salt, if using natural mussels

2 tablespoons extra-virgin olive oil

1 cup (8 fl oz/250 ml) full-bodied dry white wine such as Sauvignon Blanc

¼ teaspoon freshly ground pepper

3 tablespoons unsalted butter, cut into thin slices

Toasted French bread for serving, optional

MAKES 2 MAIN-COURSE OR
4 FIRST-COURSE SERVINGS

CHEF'S TIP
You may have heard a caution against cooking wine-based recipes in cast-iron pans. This doesn't apply here because the wine is not in contact with the cast iron for long enough to allow an exchange of flavors. Be sure to use a pan that is well seasoned and shows no signs of rust.

1 Chop the shallots, garlic, and parsley

First, dice the shallots: On a cutting board, and using a chef's knife, cut the shallots in half lengthwise and peel each half. One at a time, put the shallot halves, cut side down, on the cutting board. Alternately make a series of lengthwise cuts, parallel cuts, and then crosswise cuts to create ¼-inch (6-mm) dice. If you need help dicing shallots, turn to page 32. Next, place the garlic cloves on the cutting board, firmly press against them with the flat side of the chef's knife, and pull away and discard the papery skins. Rock the knife blade up and down and back and forth to finely chop the garlic. If you are not sure how to chop garlic, turn to page 33. Finally, rinse and pat dry the parsley sprigs. Separate the leaves from the stems, gather the leaves in a pile on the board, and rock the chef's knife over the board to chop the leaves; you should have about 3 tablespoons. For more information on chopping herbs, turn to page 35.

2 Clean the mussels

There are two kinds of mussels on the market, farm raised and natural. Natural mussels have small tough cords (called beards) that are used to attach the mollusks to the rocks or piers that are their homes. These beards must be removed before cooking. Scrub the mussels well with a sturdy brush under running cold water. If they have beards, pull them off with your fingers or a pair of well-washed pliers. Also, in order to help expel sand and grit from their systems, natural mussels should be soaked in salt water. In a large bowl, dissolve the salt in 8 cups (64 fl oz/2 l) cold water. Add the mussels and let stand for 30–60 minutes. Drain and rinse well. If a lot of sand collects at the bottom of the bowl, repeat this process. Farm-raised mussels (often raised on Prince Edward Island in Nova Scotia and labeled P.E.I. mussels) do not have beards and will not need to be soaked. Just give them a quick rinse and they're ready. Discard any mussels whose shells are cracked, or that fail to close to the touch.

3 Prepare the grill

If you need help setting up a grill, turn to pages 38–39. About 20 minutes before you start cooking, prepare a charcoal or gas grill for direct grilling over high heat. Place individual shallow bowls near the grill to warm from its heat, or warm them in a 200°F (95°C) oven. ⟩

4 Prepare the wine base

In a 12-inch (30-cm) cast-iron frying pan, heat the olive oil on the stove top over medium heat. Add the shallots and garlic and cook, stirring often, until the shallots soften and the garlic is fragrant, about 2 minutes. Add the wine and pepper and bring to a boil over high heat. Carefully add the mussels to the frying pan.

5 Grill the mussels

Before grilling, test the grill temperature: **IF YOU ARE USING A CHARCOAL GRILL,** hold your hand about 4 inches (10 cm) above the fire. If you can only count to 1 before pulling your hand away (very high heat), the coals are ready. **IF YOU ARE USING A GAS GRILL,** the temperature should reach 500°F (260°C) before you begin to cook. **FOR EITHER TYPE OF GRILL,** place the frying pan on the grill. Cover the grill and cook, stirring the mussels occasionally with tongs, until the shells open, about 5 minutes total.

6 Finish the sauce

Use the tongs to transfer the mussels to the warmed individual bowls, discarding any mussels that failed to open and leaving the cooking liquid in the pan. Using a thick oven mitt, remove the pan from the grill, add the parsley and butter to the pan and whisk continuously until the butter melts. The sauce will start to come together and appear a bit thicker. Taste the sauce; it should taste pleasantly briny from the mussels, with a bracing acidity from the wine, and have a bright herbal flavor from the parsley. If you used a charcoal grill, you will also taste light smoky overtones. No one flavor should be overpowering. You will likely not need to add any salt to the sauce, as it will be salty enough from the mussel cooking liquid.

7 Serve the mussels

The individual bowls will still be warm, so handle carefully. Using a large spoon, generously spoon the sauce over the mussels, making sure each person has enough broth to keep the mussels moist and to have on its own or with toasted bread, a favorite serving addition. Serve right away.

8 Maintain the grill for the next use

IF YOU ARE USING A CHARCOAL GRILL, cover it and let the coals burn out completely. **IF YOU ARE USING A GAS GRILL,** turn off the heat elements, seal the propane tank, and close the grill cover.

Grilled Shellfish Variations

The technique you learned for grilling mussels in a cast-iron frying pan in Grill-Roasted Mussels with White Wine & Shallots (page 78) can be used for other shellfish, including clams, shrimp, and oysters. Like the mussels, the first two are cooked with liquid (beer, chicken stock, and dry sherry) to create an accompanying sauce that is made right in the pan. The oysters, however, are grilled "dry," balanced on a bed of rice to keep their briny juices, or liquor, in their shells, and dabbed with a thick barbecue sauce. In all of the variations, the smoky flavor that comes from grilling over a live fire infuses the shellfish. Each variation makes 4 appetizer servings.

Grilled Clams with Beer and Bacon

Here, bacon echoes the smoky flavors provided by the fire.

Prepare a charcoal or gas grill for direct grilling over very high heat.

In a 12-inch (30-cm) cast-iron frying pan, sauté **4 slices bacon** on the stove top until crisp, about 5 minutes. Transfer to paper towels, leaving the fat in the pan. Add **1 finely diced yellow onion** and sauté until golden, about 3 minutes. Stir in **1 cup (8 fl oz/250 ml) lager beer**, **1 tablespoon whole-grain mustard**, **2 teaspoons firmly packed golden brown sugar**, and **¼ teaspoon freshly ground pepper** and bring to a boil. Add **36 cleaned and soaked littleneck clams**.

Place the pan on the grill. Cover the grill and cook, stirring occasionally, until the clam shells open, about 8 minutes. Transfer the clams to 4 warmed bowls. Discard any clams that failed to open. Leave the liquid in the pan. Off the heat, whisk **3 tablespoons unsalted butter** and **3 tablespoons chopped fresh flat-leaf (Italian) parsley** into the liquid in the pan. Pour over the clams. Crumble the bacon and sprinkle over the clams. Serve right away.

Grilled Shrimp with Chorizo

This easy Spanish-style recipe pairs nicely with a glass of chilled dry sherry.

Prepare a charcoal or gas grill for direct grilling over very high heat.

In a 12-inch (30-cm) cast-iron frying pan, heat **2 tablespoons extra-virgin olive oil** on the stove top over medium heat. Add **3½ oz (105 g) diced smoked chorizo links** and sauté until browned, 3–5 minutes. Transfer to paper towels, leaving the fat in the pan. Add **2 thinly sliced garlic cloves** and sauté for 1 minute. Stir in **¼ cup (2 fl oz/60 ml) dry sherry** and cook until reduced by half, about 30 seconds. Stir in **1 cup (8 fl oz/250 ml) Brown Poultry Stock (page 24)** or **low-sodium chicken broth** and **1½ lb (750 g) large shrimp (prawns), peeled and deveined (21–25 per lb/500 g)**.

Place the pan on the grill. Cover the grill and cook, stirring, until the shrimp turn opaque, about 5 minutes. Transfer the shrimp to 4 warmed bowls. Leave the liquid in the pan. Off the heat, whisk **3 tablespoons unsalted butter** and **3 tablespoons chopped fresh cilantro (fresh coriander)** into the liquid in the pan. Stir in the chorizo, pour over the shrimp, and serve right away.

"Barbecued" Oysters

Wherever oysters are harvested, there are ways to grill them. This is how they are served around the oyster farms north of San Francisco.

Prepare a charcoal or gas grill for direct grilling over very high heat. Have ready **12 scrubbed oysters in the shell**. Wrap one hand with a folded thick kitchen towel. Working with 1 oyster at a time, place it flat side up on the towel. Push the tip of an oyster knife between the flat lid and the cupped body. Twist the knife sharply to open the shell and then run the knife along the entire inside surface, detaching the muscle that connects the shell. Do not spill the juice. Bend the top shell backward, snapping it off at the hinge. Run the knife on the inside surface of the bottom shell to loosen the oyster, leaving it in the shell.

Fill a 12-inch (30-cm) cast-iron frying pan half full with **raw rice**. Nestle the oysters upright in the rice. Divide **¼ cup (2 fl oz/60 ml) Classic Barbecue Sauce (page 26)** among the 12 oysters.

Place the frying pan on the grill. Cover the grill and cook the oysters just until the edges begin to curl, 5–7 minutes total. Transfer the oysters in their shells to warmed plates and serve right away.

Shrimp Skewers with Barbecue Spices

Jumbo shrimp are best for the grill because they remain moist and juicy in the intense heat. A toss in oil prevents sticking to the grill. The spice rub of toasted cumin seeds, smoked paprika, and ground chipotle chiles provides a complex web of smoky elements before the shrimp even hit the fire.

1 **Soak the skewers, if needed**
You will need 4 flat metal skewers or eight 12-inch (30-cm) bamboo skewers for this recipe. If you are using bamboo skewers, soak them in water for at least 30 minutes to prevent them from burning on the grill, then drain.

2 **Peel and devein the shrimp**
Using your fingers, peel the shrimp, leaving the tail segment intact. Cut a shallow groove along the back of each shrimp with a paring knife and scrape away the dark vein. Place in a colander, rinse under running cold water, drain well, and pat dry with paper towels. Place in a large bowl.

3 **Season the shrimp**
Place the toasted cumin seeds in a mortar or electric spice grinder, let cool completely, about 10 minutes, and then crush or grind into small pieces. In a small bowl, mix together the cumin, paprika, oregano, onion powder, garlic powder, chipotle chile, salt, and black pepper until blended. Drizzle the shrimp with the olive oil, and toss well to coat the shrimp. Sprinkle with the spice rub and gently mix until the shrimp are evenly coated with the rub.

4 **Skewer the shrimp and prepare the grill**
Hold each shrimp so it naturally curls into a tight C shape and thread 6 shrimp onto each skewer, spacing them slightly apart. (If using bamboo skewers, use 2 skewers, held parallel, for skewering the 6 shrimp.) Let stand at room temperature while you prepare the grill. If you need help setting up a grill, turn to pages 38–39. About 20 minutes before you start cooking, prepare a charcoal or gas grill for direct grilling over high heat. Lightly rub the grill grate with paper towels coated with canola oil. For more details, turn to page 39.

5 **Grill and serve the shrimp**
Before grilling, test the grill temperature: **IF YOU ARE USING A CHARCOAL GRILL,** hold your hand about 4 inches (10 cm) above the fire. If you can count to 1 or 2 seconds before pulling your hand away (high heat), the coals are ready. **IF YOU ARE USING A GAS GRILL,** the temperature should reach at least 400°F (200°C) before you begin to cook. **FOR EITHER TYPE OF GRILL,** place the skewers on the grill, and cover the grill, if desired (see page 9). Cook, turning once with tongs, just until the shrimp turn slightly pink, are opaque throughout, and the spice rub is lightly toasted, 2–3 minutes per side. Transfer to a warmed platter and serve right away. (Remember to clean the grill while it is still hot.)

24 jumbo shrimp (prawns)
(16–20 shrimp per lb/500 g)

For the smoky spice rub

1¼ teaspoons cumin seeds, toasted (page 36)

1 tablespoon Spanish smoked paprika or sweet Hungarian paprika

1½ teaspoons dried oregano

½ teaspoon onion powder

½ teaspoon garlic powder

½ teaspoon ground chipotle chile or ¼ teaspoon cayenne pepper

½ teaspoon salt

½ teaspoon freshly ground black pepper

1 tablespoon extra-virgin olive oil

Canola oil for coating the grill grate

MAKES 4 SERVINGS

 CHEF'S TIP
Shrimp sizes are not standardized, so designations like jumbo, extra-large, and medium vary with each locality. The number of shrimp per pound (500 g) is a reliable way to determine their relative size. For example, if shrimp are labeled "16/20," there are between 16 and 20 shrimp in the pound.

Indirect-Heat Grilling & Smoking

Whenever you grill foods with indirect heat, they are cooked by reflected heat, much like they are in an oven. In this chapter, you will learn how to grill whole birds and large pieces of meat, including chicken, beef brisket, and pork shoulder, in the slow, even heat of a covered grill. You will also master two important ways to flavor foods cooked by indirect heat, smoking and brining.

Texas Beef Brisket

Barbecued brisket is my favorite grilled dish, as it has so many layers of flavor, from the bold spice crust, to the tangy mopping sauce, to the distinctive flavor of slow-smoked beef. Wrapping the meat in foil helps tenderize the brisket's tough muscle fibers, leaving only juicy slices of meat.

1 Soak the wood chips

Put the 8 or 9 handfuls of wood chips in a large bowl and add water to cover. Let the chips soak for 30 minutes. The wood chips will hydrate slightly, which prevents them from burning too fast and encourages the formation of smoke.

2 Trim the brisket

If the meat comes in a vacuum-packed plastic bag, open it and drain it in a sink. Rinse the brisket under running cold water and pat completely dry with paper towels. Using a boning knife or chef's knife, trim the surface fat from the brisket, leaving a layer ¼–½ inch (6–12 mm) thick. The fat helps to moisturize the meat as it cooks. For more details on trimming a roast, turn to page 37.

3 Make the spice rub and season the brisket

In a small bowl, mix together the chili powder, black pepper, garlic powder, onion powder, salt, and cayenne. Place the brisket on a rimmed baking sheet and, using your hands (wear latex gloves if your skin is sensitive), rub the mixture all over the brisket. Cover the brisket with plastic wrap and let stand at room temperature for at least 1 hour or refrigerate for up to 24 hours. If refrigerated, remove the brisket from the refrigerator 1 hour before grilling.

4 Prepare the onion and garlic for the mopping sauce

If you need help working with onions or garlic, turn to pages 32–33. First, dice the onion: On a clean cutting board, use a chef's knife to cut the onion in half lengthwise and peel each half. One at a time, place the onion halves, cut side down, on the cutting board. Alternately make a series of lengthwise cuts, parallel cuts, and then crosswise cuts to create ¼-inch (6-mm) dice. Be sure to stop just short of the root end; it holds the onion together as you cut. Next, mince the garlic: Put the garlic cloves on a cutting board, press firmly against them with the flat side of the chef's knife, and pull away and discard the papery skins. Rock the knife blade up and down and back and forth over the garlic to mince it.

5 Simmer the mopping sauce

In a saucepan, heat the oil over medium heat. When the oil begins to simmer, add the onion and cook, stirring often, until softened, about 3 minutes. Add the garlic and cook, stirring, until fragrant, about 1 minute. Stir in the beer, vinegar, mustard, ketchup, Worcestershire sauce, and salt and bring to a boil. Reduce the heat to low and simmer until sauce begins to thicken, about 15 minutes. Pour into a heatproof bowl and let cool completely. ›

3 cups Classic Barbecue Sauce (page 26), cooled to room temperature

8 or 9 handfuls mesquite wood chips, plus 1 additional handful dry wood chips if using a gas grill

1 whole fatty beef brisket, about 8 lb (4 kg)

For the Texas spice rub

¼ cup (¾ oz/20 g) chili powder

2 tablespoons freshly ground black pepper

2 tablespoons garlic powder

1 tablespoon onion powder

2 teaspoons salt

½ teaspoon cayenne pepper

For the mopping sauce

1 yellow onion

2 cloves garlic

1 tablespoon canola oil

1 can (12 oz/375 ml) lager beer

¼ cup (2 fl oz/60 ml) cider vinegar

2 tablespoons spicy brown mustard

2 tablespoons tomato ketchup

1 tablespoon Worcestershire sauce

1 teaspoon salt

Canola oil for coating the grill grate

MAKES 10–12 SERVINGS

CHEF'S TIP

Look for whole brisket at wholesale price clubs or butcher shops. Most supermarkets carry trimmed brisket cuts that are too lean for true barbecue.

6 Prepare the grill

If you need help setting up a grill, turn to pages 38–39. Keep in mind that this cut needs to cook for a long time to reach its optimal tenderness, so make sure you have plenty of charcoal or a full propane tank. About 30 minutes before you start cooking, prepare a charcoal or gas grill for indirect grilling over medium-low heat: **IF YOU ARE USING A CHARCOAL GRILL,** first remove the grill grate and set it aside. Next, ignite the briquettes or charcoal using a chimney starter and let them burn until they are covered with white ash. Then, pour the coals into the fire bed. Finally, using long-handled tongs, spread the hot coals 2 or 3 layers deep on the right side and left side of the grill, leaving the center free of coals. Replace the grill grate in its slots. **IF YOU ARE USING A GAS GRILL,** turn on all of the heat elements as high as they will go. After 10 minutes, turn 1 or 2 elements to medium-low heat and turn the other heat element off. **FOR EITHER TYPE OF GRILL,** place a 9-by-13-inch (23-by-33-cm) aluminum foil drip pan on the unheated area of the grill and fill it half full of water. Scrub the grill grate with a wire brush to remove any traces of food. Then, lightly rub the grill grate with paper towels coated with canola oil. For more details on oiling the grill grate, turn to page 39.

7 Add the wood chips

For more information on working with wood chips, turn to page 40. Before smoking, test the grill temperature. **IF YOU ARE USING A CHARCOAL GRILL,** hold your hand about 4 inches (10 cm) above the fire. If you can count to 4 or 5 seconds before pulling your hand away (medium-low heat), the coals are ready. Sprinkle 1 handful of the soaked wood chips over the hot coals. **IF YOU ARE USING A GAS GRILL,** the temperature should reach 325°F (165°C) before you begin to cook. Place 1 handful of dry wood chips in a smoker box or an aluminum foil packet. Place the box or packet directly over a heat element, being sure to let the chips ignite. Add 1 handful of the soaked wood chips to the smoker box or foil packet with the already-lit chips.

8 Smoke the beef

Reposition the grill grate in its slots, if necessary. Place the mopping sauce near the grill for basting. Place the brisket on the grill rack over the drip pan. Cover the grill and let the brisket cook in the aromatic smoke for 3 hours, basting about every 45 minutes with the mopping sauce. This will be about 4 times. At the same 45-minute intervals, add a handful of soaked chips to the fire to keep up a head of smoke and add more charcoal to a charcoal grill to maintain a medium-low grill temperature, about 325°F (165°C). If the pan looks dry, add more water.

9 Wrap the brisket in foil

After 3 hours of smoking, use a meat fork to transfer the brisket to a large piece of aluminum foil and wrap it tightly in the foil, sealing the edges closed. Return the wrapped brisket to the grill and continue cooking, adding more charcoal and water as needed (there is no need to add more chips, as the smoke won't penetrate the foil) for 2 hours longer. ›

10 Open the foil wrapper

Next, use long-handled tongs to open up the foil to expose the beef, letting any juices run into the drip pan (be careful, as the juices are hot). Carefully move the brisket to the grill grate and discard the foil. Baste the brisket with the mopping sauce, and add more water and wood chips and more coals, if necessary. Cover the grill and cook until the brisket is very dark and crusty and very tender when prodded with a meat fork and an instant-read thermometer inserted in the thickest part of the meat reads 185°F (85°C), about 1 hour more. The total smoking-cooking time is about 6 hours. This may seem like a high temperature for meat, but tough cuts are often cooked to this point. They have lots of connective tissue and fat, which take long, slow cooking to dissolve fully. As these meats cook, the fat and tissues baste them from the inside out, resulting in a tender texture. Stop basting the meat 10 minutes before it is removed from the grill, to eliminate the possibility of bacterial transfer from the mopping sauce to the meat. Discard any remaining mopping sauce.

11 Let the brisket rest

Using a meat fork, transfer the brisket to a carving board (a cutting board with a groove around the edge to capture the meat juices). Let the brisket rest for at least 20 minutes or up to 30 minutes. This resting period gives the smoke-infused juices, which rise to the surface during cooking, an opportunity to settle and redistribute throughout the meat. While the meat rests, the temperature will rise 5°–10°F (3°–6°C). Place a serving platter near the grill to warm from its residual heat, or warm it in a 200°F (95°C) oven.

12 Clean and maintain the grill for the next use

While the brisket is resting, use a sturdy grill brush to scrub the grill grate. Carefully remove the drip pan and discard any liquid. **IF YOU ARE USING A CHARCOAL GRILL,** cover it and let the coals burn out completely. **IF YOU ARE USING A GAS GRILL,** turn off the heat elements, seal the propane tank, and close the grill cover.

13 Serve the brisket

Put the barbecue sauce in a small nonreactive saucepan and warm gently on the stove top or on the grill rack until heated through. Pour it into a small heatproof pitcher or into a bowl with a ladle. Before you carve the meat, notice the way the meat fibers are running through the roast. This is called the *grain*. Using a carving knife or chef's knife, cut the brisket across the grain into thin slices (see opposite page). There will be lean and fatty portions. Carve the entire brisket and mix the fat and the lean portions together. You may also notice a pink ring just under the exterior of the meat. This does not mean the meat is rare; rather, it is where the meat has been colored by the smoke. Serve the brisket right away on the warmed platter, with the barbecue sauce passed on the side.

Serving brisket

The traditional way to prepare brisket is to cover it with a spicy rub and then to let the wood and smoke of the grill do all the work. That basic approach has been embellished here with the addition of a mopping sauce that creates a savory glaze. Slow cooking yields tender meat that is so full of smoky flavor that little more is needed for serving except for slicing the brisket, serving it on warm plates with a drizzle of sauce, and adding a side dish.

Carve across the grain (top left)
Notice the way the meat fibers are running through the roast; this is called the *grain*. Holding the brisket steady with a meat fork, use a long slicing knife to carve it into thin slices across the grain.

Transfer to warmed plates (left)
Slide the knife under the slices and, using the meat fork to hold them steady, transfer the slices to warmed plates.

Drizzle with barbecue sauce (above)
For a more finished look and additional flavor, drizzle the sauce generously over the brisket. Pair the sliced and sauced brisket with a side dish, such as sautéed green beans.

North Carolina Pulled Pork

In the American South, pork is the barbecue meat of choice. As with beef brisket, pork shoulder is transformed by slow cooking, spice, and hickory smoke into a meal for a crowd. The thin, sweet-and-vinegary sauce with a red pepper kick may be unusual, but it is the authentic sauce of North Carolina barbecue.

1 Soak the wood chips

Put the 8 or 9 handfuls of wood chips in a large bowl and add water to cover. Let the chips soak for 30 minutes. The wood chips will hydrate slightly, which prevents them from burning too fast and encourages the formation of smoke.

2 Trim the pork shoulder

If the pork shoulder comes in a vacuum-packed plastic bag, open it and drain it in a sink. Rinse the shoulder under running cold water and pat dry. Using a boning knife or chef's knife, trim off and discard the tough skin, leaving a 2-inch (5-cm) wide band of skin around the shank bone at the smaller end to help hold the meat together as it cooks. Next, trim the surface fat from the pork shoulder, leaving a layer ¼–½ inch (6–12 mm) thick. The fat helps to moisturize the meat as it cooks. When trimming, it is important to move the knife in slow, even strokes under the fat, pulling the fat toward you as you cut so as not to remove any of the meat. For more details on trimming a roast, turn to page 37.

3 Season the pork shoulder

In a small bowl, mix together the spice rub and salt. Place the shoulder on a rimmed baking sheet and, using your hands (wear latex gloves if your skin is sensitive), rub the spice mixture all over the pork shoulder. Be sure to cover all areas of the meat and fat for even seasoning. Cover the pork shoulder with plastic wrap and let stand at room temperature for at least 1 hour, or refrigerate for up to 24 hours. If refrigerated, remove the pork from the refrigerator 1 hour before grilling. Taking the chill off the meat will help it cook more evenly. ▸

8 or 9 handfuls hickory wood chips, plus 1 additional handful dry wood chips if using a gas grill

1 bone-in pork shoulder (picnic shoulder), 9–10 lb (4.5–5 kg)

3 tablespoons Basic Spice Rub (page 22)

1 teaspoon salt

Canola oil for coating the grill grate

2 bottles or cans (12 oz/375 ml each) cola-flavored carbonated beverage

For the North Carolina barbecue sauce

1 cup (8 fl oz/250 ml) distilled white vinegar

2 tablespoons tomato ketchup

2 cloves garlic, minced (page 33)

3 tablespoons sugar

1 teaspoon red pepper flakes

MAKES 10–12 SERVINGS

CHEF'S TIP

Brisket, pork ribs, and pork shoulder are considered the Big Three of American barbecue. Texas claims the brisket, and both Memphis and Kansas City the ribs. But it's only in North Carolina where you will find authentic pulled pork.

4 Prepare the grill

If you need help setting up a grill, turn to pages 38–39. About 30 minutes before you start cooking, prepare a charcoal or gas grill for indirect grilling over medium-low heat: **IF YOU ARE USING A CHARCOAL GRILL,** first remove the grill grate. Next, ignite the briquettes and/or charcoal using a chimney starter. Let burn until covered with white ash. Then, pour the coals into the fire bed. Spread the hot coals 2 or 3 layers deep on the right side and left side of the grill, leaving the center free of coals. Replace the grill grate in its slots. **IF YOU ARE USING A GAS GRILL,** turn on all of the heat elements as high as they will go. After 10 minutes, turn 1 or 2 elements to medium-low heat and turn the other heat element off. **FOR EITHER TYPE OF GRILL,** place a 9-by-13-inch (23-by-33-cm) aluminum foil drip pan on the unheated area of the grill and fill it half full of water. Rub the grill grate with paper towels coated with canola oil. For more details on oiling the grill grate, turn to page 39.

5 Add the wood chips

For more information on working with wood chips, turn to page 40. Before smoking, test the grill temperature. **IF YOU ARE USING A CHARCOAL GRILL,** hold your hand about 4 inches (10 cm) above the fire. If you can count to 4 or 5 seconds before pulling your hand away (medium-low heat), the coals are ready. Sprinkle 1 handful of the soaked wood chips over the hot coals. **IF YOU ARE USING A GAS GRILL,** the temperature should reach 325°F (165°C) before you begin to cook. Place 1 handful of dry wood chips in a smoker box or an aluminum foil packet. Place directly over a heat element being sure to let the chips ignite. Add 1 handful of the soaked wood chips to the smoker box or foil packet with the already-lit chips.

6 Smoke the pork

Pour the cola into a heatproof bowl. Place the pork shoulder over the drip pan, cover the grill, and let smoke for 3 hours. Every 45 minutes, add more chips and charcoal to the fire to maintain the heat level, 325°F (165°C). After 3 hours, generously baste the pork with the cola at the same 45-minute intervals and add more water to the drip pan if it looks dry. Continue to cook for 5½–6 hours total.

CHEF'S TIP

Be sure to have plenty of charcoal or a full propane tank, as a cut such as this is very tough and requires a long cooking time to tenderize.

7 Test pork for doneness and let it rest

To test for doneness, insert an instant-read thermometer into the thickest part of the meat. When done, the thermometer should read 185°F (85°C). This may seem like a high temperature, but tough cuts such as pork shoulder require long, slow cooking to tenderize fully. For more information on checking pork for doneness, turn to page 43. Using a meat fork, transfer the pork shoulder to a carving board (a cutting board with grooves around the edge to capture the meat juices). Let rest for 20–30 minutes. This resting period gives the smoky juices an opportunity to redistribute throughout the meat. While the meat rests, the temperature will rise 5°–10°F (3°–6°C).

CHEF'S TIP

Pork shoulder, sometimes called cala *or* pernil, *is a popular cut with Latino cooks. If you have trouble finding it at your neighborhood supermarket, seek it out at groceries and butchers with a Spanish-speaking clientele.*

8 Make the barbecue sauce

At least 1 hour before the pork is done, make the sauce. In a nonreactive bowl, whisk together the vinegar, ketchup, garlic, sugar, and red pepper flakes until the sugar is dissolved. Pour the sauce through a funnel into a glass bottle and let stand at room temperature. Meanwhile, put individual plates near the grill to warm from its residual heat, or warm them in a 200°F (95°C) oven.

9 Clean and maintain the grill for the next use

While the pork shoulder is resting, use a sturdy grill brush to scrub the grill grate. Carefully remove the drip pan and discard any liquid. **IF YOU ARE USING A CHARCOAL GRILL,** cover it and let the coals burn out completely. **IF YOU ARE USING A GAS GRILL,** turn off the heat elements, seal the propane tank, and close the grill cover.

10 Pull the meat into shreds

Using 2 large serving forks (not meat forks, which will not provide enough traction), pull the meat apart in opposite directions, creating large shreds. (Or, use a large knife to cut the meat, then pull it apart or chop it finely with the knife.) Serve the pulled pork hot, with the barbecue sauce on the side.

Serving ideas

A whole pork shoulder provides enough meat for up to twelve people. But even if you are not serving a crowd, it is worth it to slow smoke this flavorful meat. You can reheat the shredded pork the next day in a 250°F (120°C) oven and serve it with potatoes and your favorite side dish or combine it with coleslaw in a hearty sandwich. Or, you can use it as topping for pizza, along with barbecue sauce and a good melting cheese.

Pulled pork with potatoes and chard (top left)
Highlight the southern roots of pulled pork by serving it with mashed potatoes and garlicky sautéed Swiss chard.

Pulled pork sandwich with coleslaw (left)
Another favorite way to serve pulled pork is to pile it on a sandwich bun and drizzle it generously with the sauce. Top with a large spoonful of your favorite coleslaw.

Pizza with pulled pork and red onion (above)
For an interesting pizza, top the dough with Classic Barbecue Sauce (page 26), shredded cheese such as Monterey jack or mozzarella, pulled pork, and sliced red onion.

Barbecued Beef Ribs

These ribs, cut from a standing rib roast, are first coated with a bold spice rub, then slow smoked over a mesquite fire until tender. While delicious on their own, you can also brush these ribs with a tomato-based barbecue sauce near the end of cooking for an extra layer of old-fashioned barbecue flavor.

4 or 5 handfuls mesquite wood chips, plus 1 additional handful dry wood chips if using a gas grill

6 lb (3 kg) beef ribs

For the chili spice rub

¼ cup (¾ oz/20 g) chili powder

2 tablespoons smoked Spanish paprika or sweet Hungarian paprika

2 tablespoons freshly ground black pepper

2 tablespoons garlic powder

1 tablespoon onion powder

2 teaspoons salt

½ teaspoon cayenne pepper

Canola oil for coating the grill grate

3 cups Classic Barbecue Sauce (page 26), optional

MAKES 4 SERVINGS

CHEF'S TIP

For the best barbecued beef ribs, buy wide beef ribs cut from a rib roast. Do not buy skinny rib-bone trimmings from the thin end of the rib cage, which have little meat. Also, avoid chunky short ribs or cross-cut short ribs, also called flanken. They are very tough and thus require a moist-heat cooking method such as braising.

1 **Soak the wood chips**
Put the 4 or 5 handfuls of wood chips in a large bowl and add water to cover. Let the chips soak for 30 minutes. The wood chips will hydrate slightly, which prevents them from burning too fast and encourages the formation of smoke.

2 **Prepare the beef ribs**
Beef ribs are usually cut crosswise into 3-inch (7.5-cm) lengths. The bones that were nearest to the actual rib roast will be meatier than the ones that come from farther down the rib cage. Packaged ribs from wholesale price clubs often contain both types, and they do not require separate cooking times. If necessary, cut the ribs into 4- or 5-rib slabs.

3 **Make the spice rub and season the beef ribs**
In a small bowl, mix together the chili powder, paprika, black pepper, garlic powder, onion powder, salt, and cayenne. Using your hands (wear latex gloves if your skin is sensitive), rub the mixture all over the slabs. Place the ribs on a rimmed baking sheet and cover with plastic wrap. Let stand at room temperature for at least 1 hour or refrigerate for up to 24 hours. If refrigerated, remove the ribs from the refrigerator 1 hour before grilling. Taking the chill off the meat will help it cook more evenly.

4 **Prepare the grill**
If you need help setting up a grill, turn to pages 38–39. About 30 minutes before you start cooking, prepare a charcoal or gas grill for indirect grilling over medium-low heat: **IF YOU ARE USING A CHARCOAL GRILL,** first remove the grill grate and set it aside. Next, ignite the briquettes and/or charcoal using a chimney starter and let them burn until they are covered with white ash. Then, pour the coals onto the fire bed. Finally, using long-handled tongs, spread the hot coals 2 or 3 layers deep on the right side and left side of the grill, leaving the center free of coals. Replace the grill grate in its slots. **IF YOU ARE USING A GAS GRILL,** turn on all of the heat elements as high as they will go. After 10 minutes, turn 1 or 2 elements to medium-low heat and turn the other heat element off. **FOR EITHER TYPE OF GRILL,** place a 9-by-13-inch (23-by-33-cm) aluminum foil drip pan on the unheated area of the grill and fill it half full of water. Scrub the grill grate with a wire brush to remove any traces of food. Rub the grate with paper towels coated with canola oil. For more details on oiling the grill grate, turn to page 39. ›

5 Smoke the ribs

For more information on working with wood chips, turn to page 40. Before grilling, test the grill temperature: **IF YOU ARE USING A CHARCOAL GRILL,** hold your hand about 4 inches (10 cm) above the fire. If you can count to 4 or 5 seconds before pulling your hand away (medium-low heat), the coals are ready. Sprinkle 1 handful of the soaked wood chips over the hot coals. **IF YOU ARE USING A GAS GRILL,** the temperature should reach 325°F (165°C) before you begin to cook. Place 1 handful of the dry wood chips in a smoker box or an aluminum foil packet. Place the box or packet directly over a heat element, being sure to let the chips ignite. Add 1 handful of the soaked wood chips to the smoker box or packet with the already-lit chips. **FOR EITHER TYPE OF GRILL,** arrange the rib slabs, meaty side down, over the foil drip pan. They may overlap. Cover the grill and let the ribs smoke until the slabs are fork-tender and the meat begins to pull back from the bone, about 1½ hours. Add more charcoal and wood chips about every 30 minutes to keep the grill smoking with an average grill temperature of low, or about 300°F (150°C). This will be about 3 times. Add more hot water to the drip pan if it looks dry.

6 Apply the barbecue sauce, if desired

If you like your ribs "wet," that is, glazed with barbecue sauce, do the following: Transfer the slabs to the warmed platter. **IF YOU ARE USING A CHARCOAL GRILL,** remove the grill grate and add about 3 lb (1.5 kg) charcoal to the fire. Let the coals burn until you have a medium fire, about 30 minutes. When ready, you should be able to hold your hand about 4 inches (10 cm) above the coals and count to 3 or 4 before pulling it away. **IF YOU ARE USING A GAS GRILL,** adjust the temperature controls on all elements of the grill to 350°F (180°C). **FOR EITHER TYPE OF GRILL,** oil the grill grate. Place the slabs over the fire and brush with the sauce. Turn the slabs and cover. Grill until the barbecue sauce on the undersides of the slabs is thick and shiny, about 3 minutes. Brush the tops of the slabs, turn, and re-cover. Again, grill until the barbecue sauce on the undersides of the slabs is thick and shiny, about 3 minutes more.

7 Let the slabs rest

Transfer the slabs to a cutting board and let rest for 5–10 minutes. Place a clean serving platter or individual plates near the grill to warm from its residual heat, or warm in a 200°F (95°C) oven.

8 Clean and maintain the grill for the next use

While the slabs are resting, use a sturdy grill brush to scrub the grill grate. Carefully remove the drip pan and discard any liquid. **IF YOU ARE USING A CHARCOAL GRILL,** cover it and let the coals burn out completely. **IF YOU ARE USING A GAS GRILL,** turn off the heat elements, seal the propane tank, and close the grill cover.

9 Serve the ribs

Using a chef's knife, cut the meat between the bones into individual ribs. Serve right away on the warmed platter or plates.

Barbecued Ribs Variations

In Barbecued Beef Ribs (page 98), you learned how to use the leisurely low heat and steady aromatic smoke of indirect grilling and a flavorful barbecue sauce to produce tender, juicy beef ribs. You can use these same basic techniques to barbecue pork spareribs and baby back ribs, which come from two different parts of the pig and here are treated to two different barbecue sauces. Country-style ribs, from yet another part of the pig, require precooking in the oven to tenderize them and then only a short stint in a covered grill to brown them and give a light smoky taste. Each variation makes 4–6 servings.

Barbecued Spareribs with Mustard Sauce

Cut from the belly of the pig, spareribs have a nice proportion of meat to bone. The mustard sauce is a change from the familiar tomato-based version.

Season 6 lb (3 kg) pork spareribs, cut into 4- or 5-rib slabs, with 1 tablespoon salt and 1 teaspoon freshly ground pepper. Cover and let stand for 1 hour. Meanwhile, soak 3 or 4 handfuls hickory wood chips in water for about 30 minutes.

Prepare a charcoal or gas grill for indirect grilling over medium-low heat. Place a drip pan half full of water in the unheated area of the grill and add a handful of smoke chips. Oil the grill grate. Put the ribs on the grill over the drip pan, cover, and cook, adding more charcoal or soaked wood chips in 30-minute intervals, until the meat is fork-tender, 2½–3 hours.

Following the directions in step 6, apply 3½ cups (28 fl oz/875 ml) Mustard & Rosemary Barbecue Sauce (page 28) to the ribs.

Transfer the rib slabs to a cutting board and let rest for 5–10 minutes. Cut the slabs into individual ribs and serve right away.

Barbecued Baby Back Ribs

Baby back ribs are very tender and take the least time to cook of all the rib options. There is less meat on the bones, so you need more per serving. But the taste is well worth it.

Rub 6 lb (3 kg) baby back ribs, cut into 4- or 5-rib slabs, with 1 batch Basic Spice Rub (page 22). Cover and let stand for 1 hour. Meanwhile, soak 4 or 5 handfuls hickory wood chips in water to cover for about 30 minutes.

Prepare a charcoal or gas grill for indirect grilling over medium-low heat. Place a drip pan half full of water in the unheated area of the grill and add a handful of smoke chips. Oil the grill grate. Put the ribs on the grill over the drip pan, cover, and cook, adding more charcoal or soaked wood chips in 30-minute intervals, until the meat is fork-tender, 1½–2 hours. If you like "wet" ribs, follow the instructions in step 6, using 3 cups (24 fl oz/750 ml) Classic Barbecue Sauce (page 26).

Transfer the rib slabs to a cutting board and let rest for 5–10 minutes. Cut the slabs into individual ribs and serve right away.

Herbed Country-Style Ribs

This cut benefits from precooking to tenderize the meat before grilling. With this aromatic herb rub, there is no need for a sauce.

In a bowl, mix together 2 teaspoons dried rosemary, 2 teaspoons dried basil, 2 teaspoons dried oregano, 2 teaspoons salt, ¾ teaspoon garlic powder, and ¾ teaspoon freshly ground pepper. Rub 6 lb (3 kg) country-style ribs with the herb mixture. Cover and let stand for 1 hour.

Position a rack in the center of the oven and preheat the oven to 350°F (180°C). Spread the ribs in a large, deep roasting pan (they can overlap) and cover tightly with aluminum foil. Roast the ribs until they are almost tender, about 1¼ hours. Discard the liquid in the pan.

Prepare a charcoal or gas grill for indirect grilling over medium-low heat. Place a drip pan half full of water in the unheated area of the grill. Oil the grill grate. Place the ribs on the grill over the drip pan and cover. Cook, turning occasionally, until the ribs are browned and tender, about 20 minutes. Transfer the ribs to a cutting board and let rest for 5–10 minutes. Serve right away.

Cider-Brined Pork Loin with Herb Crust

This juicy pork roast, enhanced by a cider brine and encrusted with Dijon mustard and fresh herbs, is an example of how well-chosen ingredients and careful cooking can combine to make extraordinary eating. Note that I specify a bone-in roast. Meat cooked on the bone is juicer and more flavorful than boneless cuts.

1 Brine the pork
In a 3-qt (3-l) heatproof bowl, mix together the hot water, salt, brown sugar, rosemary, sage, peppercorns, and fennel seeds until the salt and sugar are dissolved. Add the cider and ice water and stir until the ice dissolves. Next, place the pork in a deep nonreactive pot. Pour the brine over the pork. Place a large plate on the pork to keep it submerged in the brine. Cover the pot and refrigerate for at least 18 hours or up to 24 hours.

2 Prepare the pork roast
Remove the pork from the brine and pat dry with paper towels. Spread the mustard over the meaty part and ends of the roast. Mix the rosemary, sage, and parsley in a small bowl. Sprinkle the herbs evenly over the mustard-painted areas of the pork, then let stand at room temperature while you prepare the grill.

3 Prepare the grill and cook the pork
If you need help setting up a grill, turn to pages 38–39. About 30 minutes before you start cooking, prepare a charcoal or gas grill for indirect grilling over medium heat. IF YOU ARE USING A CHARCOAL GRILL, sprinkle 1 handful of soaked chips on the coals. IF YOU ARE USING A GAS GRILL, place the dry chips in a smoker box or an aluminum foil packet and ignite them over a heat element. Add 1 handful of soaked chips to the already-lit chips. FOR EITHER TYPE OF GRILL, rub the grill grate with paper towels coated with canola oil; for more details on oiling the grill grate, turn to page 39. Place the pork, bone side down, over the drip pan. Cover the grill and cook until an instant-read thermometer inserted in the thickest part of the roast not touching the bone reads 145°–150°F (63°–65°C), about 2 hours. Add more charcoal and wood chips in 3 or 4 additions to keep the grill smoking with an average grill temperature of about 325°F (165°C).

4 Let the roast rest
Transfer the roast to a carving board, bone side down. Let rest for at least 10 minutes or up to 20 minutes. While the meat rests, the temperature will rise 5°–10°F (3°–6°C). (Remember to clean the grill while it is still hot.)

5 Serve the roast
For smaller servings, cut the rib section away from the meaty part of the roast in one piece. Set the ribs aside and save for another use. Cut the boneless roast crosswise into ½-inch (12-mm) slices. For more substantial servings, cut the ribs between the bones into chops. In either case, serve right away on warmed plates.

For the cider brine

3 cups (24 fl oz/750 ml) hot water

⅓ cup (2⅔ oz/85 g) table salt

⅓ cup (2½ oz/75 g) firmly packed golden brown sugar

3 tablespoons chopped fresh rosemary

3 tablespoons chopped fresh sage

2 tablespoons whole peppercorns

2 teaspoons fennel seeds

4 cups (32 fl oz/1 l) apple cider

3 cups (24 fl oz/750 ml) ice water

1 center-cut bone-in pork loin roast, about 4½ lb (2.25 kg), trimmed, chine bone removed and backbone cracked by the butcher

3 tablespoons Dijon mustard

1½ tablespoons chopped fresh rosemary (page 35)

1½ tablespoons chopped fresh sage (page 35)

1½ tablespoons chopped fresh flat-leaf (Italian) parsley (page 35)

4 or 5 handfuls wood chips, preferably apple or oak, plus 1 additional handful dry chips if using a gas grill

Canola oil for coating the grill grate

MAKES 6 SERVINGS

CHEF'S TIP
You may be surprised by the large amount of salt in the brine, but it is essential. The salt penetrates the meat, which draws in moisture and other flavors and tenderizes the roast.

Herb-Brined Whole Chicken

Poultry has little fat in its flesh and can easily lose flavor in the dry heat of a grill. To provide extra moisture, brine the bird, allowing it to soak up the seasoned water, which remains entrapped in the flesh after it is removed from the liquid. The result is a flavorful, juicy bird, from breast to thigh to drumstick.

1 Make the brine
At least 8 hours before you plan to grill, in a large saucepan, combine the water, salt, brown sugar, rosemary, thyme, fennel seeds, peppercorns, and bay leaves. Bring to a boil over high heat, stirring often to dissolve the salt and sugar. Reduce the heat to low and simmer for 10 minutes to draw the flavor from the herbs and spices.

2 Cool the brine
Pour the brine into a large nonreactive pot or heatproof bowl large enough to hold the chicken and the brine. Receptacles made from glass, ceramic, stainless steel, anodized aluminum, or plastic are fine, but do not use uncoated aluminum, as it may react with the salt and give the brine an off flavor. Tall containers work best, as the brine must be deep enough to submerge the chicken. Add the ice water and stir until the ice dissolves. (The brine must be very cold before using. The ice water will help drop the temperature.)

3 Add the chicken to the brine
Add the chicken to the container and submerge it in the chilled brine. Place a plate on top of the chicken to keep it under the level of the brine. Refrigerate the chicken for at least 4 hours or up to 6 hours. Use tongs occasionally to turn the chicken upside down and right side up for even distribution of the brine. Do not brine the chicken for longer than the time specified. It will not improve the flavor and texture of the bird, and, in fact, may adversely affect it, rendering it mushy and/or too salty. ›

For the herb brine

4 cups (32 fl oz/1 l) water

⅓ cup (2⅔ oz/85 g) table salt

⅓ cup (2½ oz/75 g) firmly packed golden brown sugar

1 tablespoon dried rosemary

1 tablespoon dried thyme

1 teaspoon fennel seeds

1 teaspoon peppercorns

2 bay leaves

6 cups (48 fl oz/1.5 l) ice water

1 large chicken, about 6 lb (3 kg), neck and giblets removed

Canola oil for coating the grill grate

MAKES 4 SERVINGS

4 Drain and dry the chicken

Remove the chicken from the brine. Place the chicken in a large bowl, with the body cavity opening facing down, and let the chicken drain well for 5 minutes or so. Pat the chicken completely dry with paper towels. Do not reseason the chicken. Let it stand at room temperature while you set up the grill.

5 Prepare the grill

If you need help setting up a grill, turn to pages 38–39. About 30 minutes before you start cooking, prepare a charcoal or gas grill for indirect grilling over medium-low heat: **IF YOU ARE USING A CHARCOAL GRILL,** first remove the grill grate and set it aside. Next, ignite the briquettes and/or charcoal using a chimney starter and let them burn until they are covered with white ash. Then, pour the coals onto the fire bed. Finally, using long-handled tongs, spread the hot coals 2 or 3 layers deep on the right side and left side of the grill, leaving the center free of coals. Replace the grill grate in its slots. **IF YOU ARE USING A GAS GRILL,** turn on all of the heat elements as high as they will go. After 10 minutes, turn 1 or 2 elements to medium-high heat and turn the other heat element off. **FOR EITHER TYPE OF GRILL,** place a 9-by-13-inch (23-by-33-cm) aluminum foil drip pan and fill it half full with water on the unheated area of the grill. Scrub the grill grate with a wire brush to remove any traces of food. Then, lightly rub the grill grate with paper towels coated with canola oil. For more details on oiling the grill grate, turn to page 39.

6 Cook the chicken

Before grilling, test the grill temperature: **IF YOU ARE USING A CHARCOAL GRILL,** hold your hand about 4 inches (10 cm) above the fire. If you can count to 2 or 3 seconds before pulling your hand away (medium-high heat), the coals are ready. **IF YOU ARE USING A GAS GRILL,** the temperature should reach 375°F (190°C) before you begin to cook. **FOR EITHER TYPE OF GRILL,** place the chicken, breast side up, over the drip pan. Cover the grill and cook, without turning the chicken, for 1¾ hours. Add more charcoal or adjust the temperature controls if necessary to maintain a grill temperature of medium-high, 375°–400°F (190°–200°C). >

CHEF'S TIP

Table salt has small crystals that are always the same weight per cup (about 8 oz/250 g). However, different brands of kosher salt, which has large salt flakes, range from 5 to 8 oz (155 to 250 g) per cup, which could affect the saltiness of the brine. As the type of salt really doesn't affect the flavor of the brine, I prefer to use plain, noniodized table salt for consistency.

7 Test chicken for doneness

Insert an instant-read thermometer into the thickest part of the breast. It should read 170°F (77°C). If the chicken is not done, return the chicken to the grill and cook for another 5 minutes. If you are not sure how to test poultry for doneness, turn to page 43.

CHEF'S TIP

Pork and shrimp (prawns) can also benefit from the brining technique. For pork, allow about 1 hour of soaking for every pound (500 g) of meat. For shrimp, soak for 30–45 minutes, regardless of weight.

8 Let the chicken rest

Transfer the chicken to a carving board and rest for 10–20 minutes. This brief rest before serving allows the juices to redistribute throughout the meat. While the chicken rests, the temperature will rise 5°–10°F (3°–6°C). Put individual plates near the grill to warm from its residual heat or warm in a 200°F (95°C) oven.

9 Clean and maintain the grill for the next use

While the chicken is resting, use a sturdy grill brush to scrub the grill grate. Carefully remove the drip pan and discard any liquid. **IF YOU ARE USING A CHARCOAL GRILL,** cover it and let the coals burn out completely. **IF YOU ARE USING A GAS GRILL,** turn off the heat elements, seal the propane tank, and close the grill cover.

10 Carve the chicken legs

Bracing the bird with a meat fork, use a carving knife or chef's knife to cut through the skin between the thigh and breast. Move the leg toward the board to locate the thigh joint, then cut through the joint to sever the leg. In the same way, remove the wing, cutting through the joint where it meets the breast. Cut through the joint in each leg to separate the drumstick and thigh.

11 Carve the chicken breasts

To carve each breast, make a deep horizontal base cut just above the thigh and wing joints, cutting through the breast toward the bone. Starting at the breastbone, cut downward and parallel to the rib cage, cutting the breast meat into long, thin slices. Serve the chicken on the warmed plates, asking your guests whether they prefer dark meat (leg and thigh) or white meat (breast).

Serving ideas

A brined whole chicken can be put to many uses. You can carve just the breast and pair it with a variety of side dishes, such as two summery salads, for an ideal outdoor meal. You can dice the meat and use it as the primary ingredient in a quick-and-easy lunchtime salad. And for a casual family supper, you can skip slicing the breasts when you carve the chicken, and instead serve them whole along with the other parts.

Sliced breast meat with two salads (top left)
Arrange sliced breast meat on a plate, fanning it slightly for a pretty presentation. Accompany with French-style potato salad and a tossed green salad.

Chicken salad (left)
Dice the chicken into ¾-inch (2-cm) pieces. For every ½ cup serving, mix with ½ diced celery stalk, 1 tablespoon minced red onion, and 2 tablespoons mayonnaise. Season with salt and pepper.

Family-style chicken (above)
Instead of carving the breast into slices, separate the pieces whole from the carcass. Arrange the breasts on a platter with the leg, thighs, and wings. Garnish with lemon wedges and rosemary.

Classic Grilled Chicken with Barbecue Sauce

Perfect "barbecued" chicken boasts juicy meat coated with a zesty, tomato-based sauce. This recipe, which employs a variation of indirect grilling, calls for heaping the coals in the center of the fire bed, rather than spreading them out. This will keep flare-ups to a minimum, allowing the chicken to attain a deep golden brown skin.

2 chickens, 3½–4 lb (1.75–2 kg) each, each cut into 8 serving pieces

1¼ teaspoons salt

½ teaspoon freshly ground pepper

Canola oil for coating the grill grate

1½ cups (12 fl oz/370 ml) Classic Barbecue Sauce (page 26) or Mustard & Rosemary Barbecue Sauce (page 28)

MAKES 8 SERVINGS

CHEF'S TIP

When you put chicken pieces on a hot grill, do not move them right away or the skin will tear. Wait to be sure the skin has crisped a bit and is not sticking to the grate before you turn the pieces for the first time.

1 **Prepare the chicken**
Arrange the chicken in a single layer on a rimmed baking sheet and sprinkle with the salt and pepper. Transfer the chicken to a platter, cover loosely with plastic wrap, and let stand at room temperature while you prepare the grill.

2 **Prepare the grill and cook the chicken**
If you need help setting up a grill, turn to pages 38–39. About 20 minutes before you start cooking, prepare a charcoal or gas grill for indirect grilling over high heat. **IF YOU ARE USING A CHARCOAL GRILL,** pour the ignited coals from the chimney starter into a mound in the center of the grill; do not spread them out. (You will not need a water-filled drip pan for this recipe, as the chicken does not cook for long enough to require the moisture provided by the steam.) **FOR EITHER TYPE OF GRILL,** rub the grill grate with paper towels coated with canola oil. For more details on oiling the grill grate, turn to page 39. Arrange the chicken over the unheated area of the grill and cover. The chicken fat will drip around, not onto, the fire, keeping flare-ups to a minimum. Grill for 20 minutes. Use long tongs to turn over the chicken pieces, then grill until the juices run almost clear with a slight trace of pink when pierced with a knife tip, 20–25 minutes. For more information on testing poultry for doneness, turn to page 43.

3 **Brush the chicken with the sauce**
Set aside ½ cup (4 fl oz/120 ml) of sauce for basting. Rub the hot area of the grill grate with paper towels coated with canola oil. Brush the chicken pieces with ¼ cup (2 fl oz/60 ml) of the sauce. Move the chicken directly over the hot area of the grill, cover, and cook until the sauce is glazed, about 3 minutes. Turn over the chicken pieces and brush the other sides of the chicken pieces with ¼ cup of the sauce, cover, and grill until the undersides are glazed, about 3 minutes more.

4 **Serve the chicken**
Transfer the chicken to a clean, warmed platter and serve right away, passing the remaining 1 cup (8 fl oz/250 ml) of the sauce. (Remember to clean the grill while it is still hot.)

Tea-Smoked Duck with Lemongrass Paste

Duck is so full-flavored that it can stand up to very bold seasonings. Here, soaked tea leaves, rice, and spices stand in for wood chips to make an amazingly fragrant smoke well suited to the Asian paste of lemongrass, fish sauce, and ginger that coat the outside of the bird. A complementary dipping sauce provides additional flavor.

1 Douse the duck with boiling water and quarter it

Using a heavy chef's knife, cut off the first 2 joints from both wings of the duck. Pull out the yellow pads of fat at both sides of the body cavity. Trim away any excess skin. Place the duck, breast side up, in a colander in the sink. Slowly pour about one-fourth of the boiling water over the duck. Turn the duck over and douse again with another one-fourth of the water. Repeat the dousing on both sides of the duck, then drain well and pat dry. Using the chef's knife, cut the duck lengthwise down both sides of the backbone and remove the backbone. Cut the duck in half lengthwise, cutting through the breast cartilage. Cut each duck half crosswise, separating the breast and wing from the thigh and drumstick sections.

2 Season the duck and prepare the smoke mix

In a food processor, process the lemongrass, ginger, garlic, and cilantro until finely chopped. Add the fish sauce, brown sugar, red pepper flakes, and five-spice powder and process to make a paste. Spread the paste in a thin layer all over the duck pieces. Refrigerate, uncovered, for 1–4 hours. In a bowl, combine the tea, rice, cinnamon, star anise, and water. Let steep for 5 minutes. Strain through a sieve, reserving both the liquid and the solids. Transfer the liquid to an aluminum foil drip pan; save the solids to use as wood chips.

3 Prepare the grill and smoke the duck

If you need help setting up a grill, turn to pages 38–39. About 20 minutes before you start cooking, prepare a charcoal or gas grill for indirect grilling over high heat. Place the drip pan in the unheated area of either grill. Sprinkle a handful of the smoke mix on the coals or place 1 handful of the smoke mix in a smoker box or an aluminum foil packet. Place the duck pieces, skin side up, over the drip pan. Cover the grill and let the duck cook without turning, about 35 minutes. Add the remaining tea-rice mixture. Re-cover the grill and cook until the duck skin is crisp and an instant-read thermometer inserted into the breast reads 175°F (80°C), about 30 minutes more. Transfer the duck to a cutting board and let stand for 5 minutes. (Remember to clean the grill while it is still hot.)

4 Make the dipping sauce and serve the duck

Whisk together the vinegar, granulated sugar, fish sauce, and red pepper flakes until the sugar is dissolved. Cut each duck quarter into 2 or 3 pieces. Transfer the pieces to a warmed platter and top with the cilantro sprigs. Serve right away, with the dipping sauce on the side.

1 Muscovy or Long Island duck, about 4 lb (2 kg), neck and giblets removed

2 qt (2 l) boiling water

For the lemongrass paste

2 stalks lemongrass, bulb removed, peeled, and coarsely chopped

4 slices peeled fresh ginger, each ⅛ inch (3 mm) thick

3 cloves garlic, crushed under a knife and peeled (page 33)

8 large sprigs fresh cilantro (fresh coriander)

¼ cup (2 fl oz/60 ml) fish sauce

2 tablespoons firmly packed golden brown sugar

½ teaspoon red pepper flakes

¼ teaspoon five-spice powder

For the tea-rice smoke mix

⅓ cup (1 oz/15 g) jasmine tea leaves

⅓ cup (2½ oz/75 g) long-grain rice

3 cinnamon sticks

3 star anise pods

3 cups (24 fl oz/750 ml) water

For the dipping sauce

6 tablespoons (3 fl oz/90 ml) unseasoned rice vinegar

2 tablespoons granulated sugar

1 tablespoon fish sauce

½ teaspoon red pepper flakes

Fresh cilantro (fresh coriander) sprigs for serving

MAKES 2–3 SERVINGS

Maple-Smoked Salmon Steaks with Maple-Mustard Sauce

Salmon steaks gain a smoky flavor when prepared on a home grill. A triple dose of maple, in the form of wood chips or chunks, syrup, and crystallized syrup (also called maple sugar), delivers layers of complexity. The mustard in the sauce provides a nice counterpoint to these sweet elements.

For the maple brine

¼ cup (2 oz/60 g) table salt

⅓ cup (3½ oz/105 ml) maple syrup, preferably Grade B

1 teaspoon whole peppercorns, crushed

6 cups (48 fl oz/1.5 l) ice water

6 salmon steaks, about ½ lb (250 g) each

For the maple-mustard sauce

3 tablespoons maple sugar or firmly packed golden brown sugar

2 tablespoons white wine vinegar

¼ cup (2 oz/60 g) Dijon mustard

⅓ cup (3 fl oz/80 ml) mild-flavored oil such as grapeseed or canola

1 tablespoon chopped fresh tarragon (page 35)

Canola oil for oiling the grill grate

2 or 3 handfuls maple, alder, or hickory wood chips, soaked in water for 30 minutes, plus 1 additional handful dry wood chips if using a gas grill

MAKES 6 SERVINGS

SHORTCUT

If you are short on time, and the kitchen is cool, you can air-dry the salmon outside of the refrigerator. Place the salmon, on the rack and baking sheet, on a work surface. Train an electric fan, on medium speed, directly on the salmon. The surface will become dry and shiny in about 45 minutes.

1 **Brine the salmon steaks**
In a glass or ceramic bowl, whisk together the salt, maple syrup, peppercorns, and water until the salt is dissolved, about 2 minutes. Submerge the salmon steaks in the brine, weighting them down with a plate, if necessary. Cover and refrigerate for up to 2 hours. Do not brine the salmon longer or it may become mushy or too salty.

2 **Air-dry the surface of the salmon**
Remove the salmon from the brine and rinse under running cold water. Rub your finger along the salmon flesh to make sure all of the small bones have been removed. Pat dry and place the salmon steaks on a large wire rack set over a rimmed baking sheet. Refrigerate, uncovered, until the surface of the salmon is dry and shiny, about 2 hours.

3 **Make the mustard sauce**
In a bowl, mix together the maple sugar and vinegar and let stand for 5 minutes until the sugar begins to dissolve. Add the mustard and whisk to completely dissolve the sugar. Gradually whisk in the oil. Stir in the tarragon. Cover and refrigerate for at least 1 hour or up to overnight.

4 **Prepare the grill**
If you need help setting up a grill, turn to pages 38–39. About 20 minutes before you start cooking, prepare a charcoal or gas grill for indirect grilling over medium heat. Rub the grill grate with canola oil; for more details, turn to page 39.

5 **Smoke the salmon and clean the grill**
Place the salmon steaks over the drip pan. Cover the grill and cook for 15 minutes. Add the wood chips to the coals or the smoker box. Re-cover and cook until the salmon flesh is barely opaque at the center when tested with a knife tip, about 15 minutes more. Let the salmon cool to room temperature, about 30 minutes. (Remember to clean the grill while it is still hot.)

6 **Chill and serve the salmon**
Place the salmon on a platter, cover with plastic wrap, and refrigerate until chilled, at least 2 hours or overnight. Remove the mustard sauce from the refrigerator 1 hour before serving. Serve the chilled salmon with a spoonful of the mustard sauce on the side.

Wood-Planked Salmon with Mustard-Dill Butter

Here, based on a cooking method practiced by Native Americans of the Northwest, salmon is cooked directly on cedar or alder planks. The fish is infused with the aroma of the wood, which lends a pleasing smoky flavor. An easy paste made by blending butter with grainy mustard and fresh dill melts to form a complementary sauce.

1 Soak and drain the plank(s)
Wood planks for grilling come in a variety of sizes. You may need 2 small planks to hold 4 fillets. They must be well soaked before using, as dry planks will burn and scorch. In a baking dish or in a sink, soak the plank(s) in cold water to cover for at least 2 hours or up to overnight before grilling. Drain well.

2 Marinate the salmon
Rinse the salmon and pat dry. Rub your fingers over the fillets and, using small fish tweezers, remove any small bones you detect. In a shallow ceramic or glass dish, whisk together the wine, oil, garlic, salt, and pepper. Place the salmon in the marinade, skin side up, cover tightly, and refrigerate for 30–60 minutes. Do not marinate the fish longer or it may become mushy.

3 Make the mustard-dill butter
Meanwhile, in a small bowl, using a small rubber spatula, mix together the butter, mustard, dill, and salt until well mixed and smooth. Cover and let stand at room temperature while cooking the salmon.

4 Prepare the grill and cook the salmon
If you need help setting up a grill, turn to pages 38–39. About 20 minutes before you start cooking, prepare a charcoal or gas grill for indirect grilling over medium heat. Place the drained plank(s) over the hottest part of the fire and leave there until the edges begin to char, about 2 minutes. Turn over the planks and leave there for about 2 more minutes to char the other side. Move the plank(s) to the cool side of the grill, over the drip pan, and arrange the salmon fillets on top, skin side down. Cover and grill until the salmon flesh is barely opaque when flaked with the tip of a sharp knife, about 20 minutes. If it is flaking without being prodded, it is overdone. If you are unsure how to test fish for doneness, turn to page 43.

5 Serve the salmon
Transfer each fillet to a warmed dinner plate and serve with a generous dollop of the mustard-dill butter. Serve right away. (Remember to clean the grill while it is still hot.)

1 large or 2 small untreated cedar or alder planks for grilling

4 skin-on salmon fillets, 6–7 oz (185–220 g) each

For the marinade

½ cup (4 fl oz/125 ml) full-bodied dry white wine such as Sauvignon Blanc

¼ cup (2 fl oz/60 ml) canola oil

1 clove garlic, minced

¼ teaspoon salt

¼ teaspoon freshly ground pepper

For the mustard-dill butter

6 tablespoons (3 oz/90 g) unsalted butter, softened

1 tablespoon whole-grain mustard

1 tablespoon finely chopped fresh dill (page 35)

⅛ teaspoon salt

MAKES 4 SERVINGS

CHEF'S TIP
Wood-plank grilling is not only limited to fish. You can use this method to cook meat and poultry as well. For extra aroma, sprinkle some garlic or sliced onion around the plank. Their flavors will infuse the grilled food.

5

Grilled Vegetables
& Fruit

The high heat of the grill brings out the inherent sweetness
of fruits and vegetables, while keeping their flavors fresh
and natural. Here, you will see how to cook ratatouille, a
stove-top favorite, on the grill; how to start potatoes on
the stove top and finish them on the grill; and how grilled
corn and stone fruits, both cooked in just minutes, are
easily dressed up with a flavored butter.

Grilled Ratatouille

Ratatouille, the famed French vegetable ragout, is traditionally simmered on top of the stove. Here, the vegetables are grilled, which intensifies the flavor of each and brings them all together in a deliciously smoky finish. The grill marks visible on the vegetables contribute to an eye-catching presentation.

1 Crush the garlic
Place the garlic cloves on the cutting board, firmly press against them with the flat side of a chef's knife, and pull away and discard the papery skins. If you need help peeling the garlic, turn to page 33.

2 Make the garlic oil
In a small saucepan over low heat, combine the oil and garlic. Heat until small bubbles surround the garlic cloves and they turn golden brown, about 5 minutes. Remove from the heat and let stand for 10 minutes to infuse the oil further with garlic flavor. Using a slotted spoon, remove the garlic from the oil and discard it. Place the saucepan with the infused oil near the grill.

3 Prepare the eggplant
Using a serrated knife, trim the green top off the eggplant, then cut the eggplant crosswise into slices ½ inch (12 mm) thick. Sprinkle 1 teaspoon of the salt over both sides of the eggplant slices. Place a large colander in the sink and add the eggplant slices. Let the eggplant stand, allowing the juices to drain into the sink, for at least 30 minutes or up to 1 hour. The eggplant slices will have softened and will not be as shiny as when they were first cut. The method of salting the eggplant removes some of the bitter juices and improves its flavor and texture.

4 Prepare the onion
It takes time for an onion to be grilled until fork-tender. Wrapping the onion in foil provides a moist cooking environment that aids in softening. Use a chef's knife to cut the top and bottom ½ inch (12 mm) from the onion. Remove the papery peel. Cut the onion crosswise into rounds ¼–½ inch (6–12 mm) thick. Lightly brush a 12-inch (30-cm) square of aluminum foil with canola oil and arrange the onion slices in their original sequence to make a relatively round sphere in the center of the oiled foil. Drizzle the slices with 2 teaspoons of the garlic oil, ⅛ teaspoon of the salt, and the black pepper and gather the foil to enclose the onion. Set aside. ❯

For the garlic oil

4 cloves garlic

½ cup (4 fl oz/125 ml) extra-virgin olive oil

1 large globe eggplant (aubergine), about 1½ lb (750 g)

1⅛ teaspoons plus ½ teaspoon salt

1 large yellow onion

Canola oil for coating the foil and the grill grate

⅛ teaspoon freshly ground black pepper

2 zucchini (courgettes), about 1 lb (500 g) total weight

2 large red bell peppers (capsicums)

3 large tomatoes, about 1 lb (500 g) total weight

½ cup (½ oz/15 g) fresh basil leaves

¼ teaspoon red pepper flakes

MAKES 4–6 SERVINGS

CHEF'S TIP
Flavored oils are a great way to add flavor to vegetables. Homemade versions are best when used the day they are made, as they do not refrigerate well.

5

7

It is not necessary to peel the eggplant and zucchini for grilling. Any bitterness in the skin is a welcome counterpoint to the sweet taste of the peppers and onions. It will also add a rustic look and flavor to the ratatouille.

5 Prepare the remaining vegetables

First, cut the zucchini: Trim the top and bottom from the zucchini, then cut each in half lengthwise. Next, prepare the bell peppers: Working with 1 pepper at a time and using a paring knife, cut around the stem and discard it. Cut a long slit down the side of the pepper, then open it up so it lies flat on the cutting board. Cut ½ inch (12 mm) from the top and bottom. Cut out and discard the ribs and seeds. Then, ready the tomatoes: Cut each tomato in half crosswise through its equator. Finally, rinse the eggplant slices: Rinse the slices well under running cold water to remove the salt. Pat them completely dry with paper towels. Arrange all the vegetables on a baking sheet. Place serving plates near the grill to warm from its heat, or warm them in a 200°F (95°C) oven.

6 Prepare the grill

If you need help setting up a grill, turn to pages 38–39. About 20 minutes before you start cooking, prepare a charcoal or gas grill with 2 areas of high heat and 1 cooler area: **IF YOU ARE USING A CHARCOAL GRILL,** first remove the grill grate and set it aside. Next, ignite the briquettes and/or charcoal using a chimney starter and let them burn until they are covered with white ash. Then, pour the coals into the fire bed. Finally, using long-handled tongs, spread the hot coals 2 or 3 layers deep in one-third of the fire bed and 1 or 2 layers deep in another third of the fire bed, leaving the remaining third free of coals. Replace the grill grate. **IF YOU ARE USING A GAS GRILL,** turn on all of the heat elements as high as they will go. **FOR EITHER TYPE OF GRILL,** scrub the grill grate with a wire brush to remove any traces of food. Then, lightly rub the grill grate with paper towels coated with canola oil. For more details on oiling the grill grate, turn to page 39.

7 Grill the onion and peppers

Before grilling, test the grill temperature: **IF YOU ARE USING A CHARCOAL GRILL,** hold your hand about 4 inches (10 cm) above the hottest part of the fire. If you can count only to 1 or 2 seconds before pulling your hand away (high heat), the coals are ready. **IF YOU ARE USING A GAS GRILL,** leave 1 or 2 heat elements on high and turn the other heat element to medium. The temperature should reach at least 425°F (220°C) before you begin to cook. **FOR EITHER TYPE OF GRILL,** place the onion over the cooler area of the grill. Place the peppers skin down over the hottest part of the grill. Grill until the pepper skins are blackened, 8–10 minutes. Transfer the peppers to a bowl to cool while you grill the other vegetables.

8 Grill the remaining vegetables

Brush the eggplant, zucchini, and tomatoes on both sides with half of the remaining garlic oil and place on the grill. Grill the tomatoes, cut side up, until the skins blister, about 3 minutes. Turn over and cook just until the cut sides are marked by the grill, about 2 minutes more. Transfer to a platter. Grill the eggplant and zucchini, turning once, until marked by the grill and tender when pierced with a paring knife, about 8 minutes total. Transfer to a platter. ›

9 Check the onion for tenderness

Carefully unwrap the onion and pierce it with a paring knife to check if the slices are tender. The knife should be able to pierce easily, but the onion should not be too soft, as it may continue to cook once it is removed from the grill. If the slices are still tough, rewrap them in the foil and continue cooking for 2–3 minutes. Remove the onion slices from the foil and transfer to the platter.

10 Peel and chop the vegetables and mix the ratatouille

Transfer the grilled vegetables to a cutting board. Pour any vegetable juices that may have collected on the platter into a large bowl. Peel off and discard the blistered skins from the peppers and tomatoes. Next, use a chef's knife to chop the peppers, tomatoes, eggplant, zucchini, and onion slices into ½–¾-inch (12-mm–2-cm) chunks and place in the large bowl. Then, tear the basil leaves into small pieces and add them to the bowl with red pepper flakes and the remaining garlic oil and ½ teaspoon salt. Mix gently. Let stand for 20 minutes, to allow the flavors to come together.

11 Clean and maintain the grill for the next use

While the ratatouille is standing, scrub the grill grate with a sturdy grill brush. **IF YOU ARE USING A CHARCOAL GRILL,** cover it and let the coals cool completely. **IF YOU ARE USING A GAS GRILL,** turn off the heat elements, seal the propane tank, and close the grill cover.

12 Adjust the seasonings

The ratatouille can be served at room temperature. If you wish to serve it hot, warm the ratatouille in a large frying pan over medium heat, stirring occasionally, until just heated through, about 5 minutes. Taste the ratatouille; you should be able to taste each vegetable in the mixture, spiked by garlic, red pepper flakes, and fresh basil, and with a smoky undertone from the grill. No one flavor should be dominating. If the dish tastes a little dull, stir in a little more salt, black pepper, or red pepper flakes until the flavors are nicely balanced.

13 Serve the ratatouille

Serve the ratatouille right away on the warmed plates or let cool to room temperature.

Serving ideas

Grilling vegetables for ratatouille is one of the tastiest ways to prepare the bounty of the summer garden. But you don't have to combine these seasonal vegetables into a single dish. Grilled eggplant slices and zucchini halves are delicious on their own, dressed with garlic oil and fresh herbs. Or, you can combine bell peppers and tomatoes and toss them with capers and garlic oil for an easy, colorful salad—a perfect side dish for grilled meats.

Grilled zucchini with oregano (top left)
For a Mediterranean-style side dish, serve grilled zucchini (courgettes) with an extra drizzle of garlic oil and a sprinkle of chopped fresh oregano. This treatment is also good with yellow summer squash.

Pepper and tomato salad (left)
Combine sliced grilled peppers (capsicums) and tomatoes in a bowl with some rinsed capers. Toss with a dressing made of garlic oil, fresh lemon juice or balsamic vinegar, and salt and pepper.

Spicy grilled eggplant (above)
Sprinkle grilled eggplant (aubergine) rounds with chopped fresh basil and red pepper flakes and then drizzle with garlic oil.

Grilled Corn on the Cob with Roasted Garlic Butter

Many grilled corn recipes call for soaking and/or husking the ears before putting them on the fire. My version is simple: just throw the whole ears on the hot grill. The husks will char, lending a smokiness to the kernels, which steam inside. The garlic turns sweet on the grill, lending the butter its distinctive flavor.

For the roasted garlic butter

2 heads garlic

1 teaspoon olive oil

⅛ teaspoon salt

⅛ teaspoon freshly ground pepper

1 cup (8 oz/250 g) unsalted butter, at room temperature

8 ears corn, husks and silks intact

Salt and freshly ground pepper for serving

MAKES 6–8 SERVINGS

CHEF'S TIP
When grilling anything wrapped in aluminum foil, take care when you remove the packet from the grill and open it. The hot steam trapped inside will escape rapidly and could burn you.

1 **Prepare the grill and prepare the garlic**
If you need help setting up a grill, turn to pages 38–39. About 20 minutes before you start cooking, prepare a charcoal or gas grill for indirect grilling over high heat. Using a chef's knife, cut the top ¼ inch (6 mm) from each garlic head. Drizzle the exposed cloves with the olive oil and sprinkle with the salt and pepper. Wrap each garlic head in aluminum foil.

2 **Grill-roast the garlic**
Before grilling, test the grill temperature: **IF YOU ARE USING A CHARCOAL GRILL,** hold your hand about 4 inches (10 cm) above the cooler part of the fire. If you can count to 3 or 4 seconds before pulling your hand away (medium heat), the coals are ready. **IF YOU ARE USING A GAS GRILL,** leave 1 or 2 heat elements on high and turn the other heat element to medium. The temperature should reach at least 375°F (190°C) before you begin to cook. **FOR EITHER TYPE OF GRILL,** place the garlic on the medium-hot area of the grill, cover, and cook until tender, about 40 minutes. Remove from the grill and let cool completely.

3 **Make the garlic butter**
Squeeze the soft flesh from the garlic into a small bowl. Mash the garlic and butter with a rubber spatula until smooth and well incorporated. Set aside.

4 **Grill the corn**
IF YOU ARE USING A CHARCOAL GRILL, add 3 lb (1.5 kg) more briquettes or charcoal to the fire and let burn until the coals are covered with white ash. Using long-handled tongs, spread the coals evenly in the fire bed. In about 10 minutes, check the grill temperature. If you can hold your hand 4 inches (10 cm) above the fire for only 1 or 2 seconds before pulling your hand away (high heat), the coals are ready. **IF YOU ARE USING A GAS GRILL,** turn all the heat elements to high. The temperature should reach 450°F (230°C) before you begin to grill. **FOR EITHER TYPE OF GRILL,** place the corn on the grill grate and cover the grill. Cook, turning occasionally, until the husks are well browned on all sides, about 20 minutes.

5 **Remove the husks and serve the corn**
Carefully transfer the corn to a cutting board. Remove the husks and silks and place the ears in a large bowl covered with aluminum foil. The kernels will be tinged golden brown. Serve the corn hot, with the roasted garlic butter, salt, and pepper on the side. (Remember to clean the grill while it is still hot.)

Grilled Potatoes with Rosemary, Lemon & Parmesan

Cooking vegetables on the grill infuses them with smoky flavor. However, in order to get firm vegetables like potatoes crisp and golden brown, they are usually parboiled first. The finishing flavors of rosemary, olive oil, lemon zest, and Parmigiano-Reggiano cheese make this a versatile side dish for roasted meats and poultry.

1 Make the rosemary-lemon oil

In a small saucepan over low heat, combine the lemon zest, rosemary sprigs, and olive oil. Once small bubbles appear around the edges of the rosemary, after about 10 minutes, remove the pan from the heat and let cool completely. Pour through a sieve into a small bowl, pressing hard against the solids to extract as much oil as possible. Cover and set aside at room temperature for up to 8 hours.

2 Parboil the potatoes

Place the potatoes in a large pot, cover with cold, salted water and bring to a boil over high heat. Uncover and reduce the heat to medium. Boil until the potatoes barely yield to the tip of a paring knife, about 12 minutes. Drain and rinse under cold water. Once cool enough to handle, cut the potatoes lengthwise into halves or quarters, depending on their size. Place in a bowl and toss with ¼ cup (2 fl oz/60 ml) of the rosemary-lemon oil. Reserve the remaining oil.

3 Prepare the grill

If you need help setting up a grill, turn to pages 38–39. About 20 minutes before you start cooking, prepare a charcoal or gas grill for direct grilling over medium heat. Have a wide spatula handy. Then lightly rub the grill grate with paper towels coated with canola oil. For more details, turn to page 39.

4 Grill the potatoes

Before grilling, test the grill temperature: **IF YOU ARE USING A CHARCOAL GRILL,** hold your hand about 4 inches (10 cm) above the fire. If you can count to 3 or 4 seconds before pulling your hand away (medium heat), the coals are ready. **IF YOU ARE USING A GAS GRILL,** leave 1 or 2 heat elements on high and turn the other heat element off. The temperature should reach 375°F (190°C) before you begin to cook. **FOR EITHER TYPE OF GRILL,** spread the potatoes on the grate and cover the grill. Grill, turning the potatoes occasionally, until golden brown, about 15 minutes. Transfer the potatoes to a warmed serving bowl.

5 Serve the potatoes

Drizzle the remaining rosemary-lemon oil over the potatoes. Add the cheese and the salt and pepper and mix gently. Taste the potatoes; you should detect all of the flavors, with no flavor dominating. If you feel the potatoes taste dull, add a small amount of salt and/or pepper and mix until the flavors are nicely balanced. Serve right away. (Remember to clean the grill while it is still hot.)

For the rosemary-lemon oil

1 large lemon, zest removed in strips with a vegetable peeler

4 sprigs fresh rosemary, each 4 inches (10 cm) long

½ cup (4 fl oz/125 ml) extra-virgin olive oil

3 lb (1.5 kg) red-skinned potatoes (about 14 medium potatoes), unpeeled and well scrubbed under running cold water

Canola oil for coating the grill grate

2-oz (60-g) chunk Parmigiano-Reggiano cheese, cut into thin shavings with a vegetable peeler

¾ teaspoon coarse salt, preferably *fleur de sel* or another finishing salt

¼ teaspoon freshly ground black pepper or red pepper flakes

MAKES 6 SERVINGS

CHEF'S TIP

When working with lemon zest (the colored part of the peel), avoid the white pith underneath, as it has a bitter flavor. If necessary, scrape the pith from the peel with a paring knife before using the zest.

Grilled Stone Fruit with Toasted Almond Butter

When summertime's stone fruits are at their best, grill them for a fast, warm dessert. I've used plums and peaches here, but apricots, nectarines, and pluots are all equally attractive candidates. The grill-marked fruits are perfectly complemented by the vanilla-scented almond butter.

For the toasted almond butter

¾ cup (3 oz/90 g) sliced (flaked) natural almonds

1 tablespoon firmly packed golden or dark brown sugar

6 tablespoons (3 oz/90 g) unsalted butter, at room temperature

½ vanilla bean

6 firm but ripe plums, halved lengthwise and pits removed

3 firm but ripe peaches, halved lengthwise and pits removed

Canola oil for coating the grill grate and brushing the fruit

MAKES 6 SERVINGS

CHEF'S TIP

After scraping the seeds from vanilla bean pods, you can reserve them to make vanilla sugar: Combine the vanilla pods and 2 cups (500 g) granulated sugar in an airtight container. Let stand at room temperature for 2 weeks so the vanilla pods can infuse the sugar. Use to flavor beverages or in baking.

1 **Toast the almonds**
Place the almonds in a dry frying pan over medium heat and toast, stirring or shaking frequently, until they smell smoky and are golden in color, 2–3 minutes. Transfer to a plate and let cool completely. For more information on toasting nuts, turn to page 36.

2 **Make the toasted almond butter**
Place ½ cup (2 oz/60 g) of the toasted almonds and the brown sugar in a food processor fitted with the metal blade. Process until the almonds are very finely chopped. Transfer to a small bowl and add the butter. Using the tip of a paring knife, cut the vanilla bean lengthwise. With the back of the paring knife, scrape the moist vanilla seeds from the pod's halves into the bowl. Mix well. Cover with plastic wrap and let stand at room temperature for up to 8 hours. (Do not refrigerate the butter; it will melt best over the hot fruit if it is soft.)

3 **Prepare the grill**
If you need help setting up a grill, turn to pages 38–39. About 20 minutes before you start cooking, prepare a charcoal or gas grill for direct grilling over medium-high heat. Then, lightly rub the grill grate with paper towels coated with canola oil. For more details on oiling the grill grate, turn to page 39.

4 **Grill the fruit**
Before grilling, test the grill temperature: IF YOU ARE USING A CHARCOAL GRILL, hold your hand about 4 inches (10 cm) above the fire. If you can count to 2 or 3 seconds before pulling your hand away (medium heat), the coals are ready. IF YOU ARE USING A GAS GRILL, turn 1 or 2 heat elements to medium-high, and turn the other heat element off. The temperature should reach 375°F (190°C) before you begin to cook. FOR EITHER TYPE OF GRILL, brush the cut sides of the plums and peaches lightly with oil and place, cut side down, on the hot part of the grill. Grill until the fruit has grill marks, 2–3 minutes. Turn and grill until the skins are beginning to blister, 2–3 minutes more.

5 **Serve the fruit**
For each serving, place 2 plum halves and 1 peach half in a dessert bowl and top with a heaping dollop of the butter. Sprinkle with the remaining ¼ cup (1 oz/30 g) toasted almonds and serve right away. (Remember to clean the grill while it is still hot.)

Using Key Tools & Equipment

While some pieces of kitchen equipment cross over from other cooking methods, quite a few of the tools you need are specialized. These include the fuel itself (be it charcoal, propane, or natural gas), utensils for building a charcoal fire, long-handled tools for manipulating food over a hot flame, materials for flavoring the food (such as wood chips and planks), and a range of accessories, from hinged grill baskets to smoker boxes.

Charcoal Grilling Equipment

A kettle-shaped charcoal grill encourages good air circulation for a healthy fire; vents in the cover and base control airflow. Look for a model with a thermometer in the cover, so you can monitor the heat level, or, insert a long, metal deep frying thermometer into the top vent. Charcoal grills come in a variety of sizes, so choose one that fits your needs. However, smaller ones may not have the capacity needed for indirect-heat grilling and smoking.

A chimney starter, a metal cylinder with a wooden handle, a base, and vents,

is by far the most efficient method for building a charcoal fire; just fill the bottom, under the base, with crumpled newspaper, fill the top chamber with the charcoal to the rim, and light the paper from underneath. The average starter holds about 5 pounds (2.5 kg) of briquettes or 3 pounds (1.5 kg) of hardwood charcoal. To estimate the amount of charcoal you need, consider it will take about 20 minutes for one chimney starter full of charcoal to burn. Long matches or a butane-fueled gas wand make lighting safe and easy.

Gas Grilling Equipment

Propane gas grills are easy to clean and maintain. Like charcoal grills, they are found in a variety of sizes and styles. If you do a lot of indirect-heat grilling and smoking, consider purchasing a larger grill, as the smaller models, with their low covers and small propane tanks, may not perform as well. Large, stationary gas grills are often supplied with natural gas from a durable home line. All propane tanks must be equipped with an overfill prevention device; if your tank is more than a few years old, replace it.

Fuels for Charcoal Grilling

Hardwood charcoal starts out very hot, then turns to ash fairly quickly. The specific types of wood processed to make hardwood charcoal (also called lump charcoal) are generally interchangeable. Charcoal briquettes, made from pulverized charcoal and binders, are pressed into uniform shapes and burn evenly and slowly. Both briquettes and hardwood charcoal are sold in bags. A mix of equal parts hardwood charcoal and briquettes is an efficient fuel option.

Flavoring Materials

Soaked wood chips are added to a grill to smolder, infusing grilling foods with a smoky flavor. Mesquite and hickory are readily available but also look for chips from fruit woods and other trees. Food cooked on cedar, maple, or alder planks will pick up the flavor of the wood.

Grilling Tools

Long-handled grilling tools—tongs, meat fork, and spatula—are ideal for handling food on the grill. Long, thick oven mitts protect against a grill's heat. A sturdy wire brush with a scraper is indispensable for cleaning the grill grate.

Grilling Accessories

To contain food that may otherwise fall through the grate, you need a hinged grill basket. Soaked bamboo or metal skewers, which are used for small pieces of food, also simplify turning. A smoker box, a gas-grill accessory, holds the smoldering wood chips that infuse the grilling food and keep any ashes from plugging the jets of the heat elements. A disposable aluminum foil pan is placed under the grill grate to catch any drippings. Liquid is added to it to provide moisture when foods are grilled for long periods.

Knives & Cutting Boards

A sharp chef's knife is the workhorse of the kitchen, essential for many jobs. A boning knife is used for many trimming jobs. Poultry shears are ideal for cutting up raw poultry before grilling. The teeth of a serrated knife efficiently cut through crusty bread and thin-skinned tomatoes. A heavy-bladed cleaver comes in handy for chopping through poultry bones. A paring knife is used to prepare vegetables and to test fish and poultry for doneness. Do your knife work on a wooden cutting board; hard plastic boards stain easily and can retain more food odors than wood.

Carving Tools

Use a long, sharp slicing or carving knife to carve grilled roasts and chicken; a two-pronged meat fork will help hold the meat steady. A grooved cutting board will catch any carving juices.

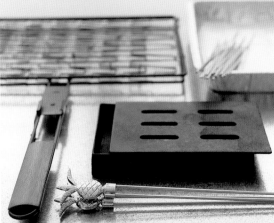

Puréeing & Grinding Tools

The sharp blade of a food processor can be used for mincing tough ingredients like lemongrass and coarsely chopping beef for burgers. The smaller bowl and blade of a blender are useful for creating puréed sauces and thick marinades. An electric coffee mill, reserved for use as a spice grinder, makes preparing spices for rubs an easy task. A mortar and pestle is an effective tool for the same job.

Saucepans & Frying Pans

To keep classic barbecue sauces from scorching, use a heavy-bottomed saucepan. A medium frying pan is perfect for sautéing onions and garlic, and you'll need a small frying pan for toasting seeds, spices, and nuts. For cooking mollusks and shellfish on the grill, a well-seasoned cast-iron frying pan is indispensable.

Other Pans & Dishes

A large, rimmed baking sheet holds food while it stands at room temperature. For homemade stocks, use an 8-quart (8-l) stockpot or Dutch oven. The same stockpot (made from a nonreactive material) or an enamel-coated pot is the perfect vessel for brining. A shallow nonreactive dish will hold foods while they marinate and can also be used to soak wooden skewers before grilling.

Bowls

You'll need a very large bowl for brining or marinating large cuts of meat and poultry. Medium bowls are used for general mixing and blending. Small bowls, or even ramekins, are perfect when creating the *mise en place* for a recipe. Nonreactive heatproof glass or stainless steel are the best materials.

Measuring Tools

Have cups for measuring dry ingredients in regular increments from ¼ cup to 1 cup. For liquid measures, 1-cup (8–fl oz/250-ml), 2-cup (16–fl oz/500-ml), and 4-cup (32–fl oz/1-l) sizes will meet all your needs. The same measuring spoons are used for both wet and dry ingredients; look for a set that ranges from ⅛ teaspoon to 1 tablespoon. For accurate quanitites when measuring recipe ingredients, do not substitute liquid measuring cups for dry measuring cups, or vice versa.

Stirring Implements

Wooden spoons and flat-bottomed spatulas are best for stirring in metal pans, as they will not scratch the surface. A heat-resistant, flexible silicone spatula easily dislodges sticky foods from hot pots, while a regular rubber spatula (not

pictured) can be used in cooler situations. Use a whisk to combine ingredients quickly. A large slotted spoon is ideal for skimming stocks.

Brushes

Reserve a basting brush for applying sauces to grilled foods. Often there is a long-handled version in grilling-tool sets that you can reserve for just that use. A pastry brush can be used to coat smaller items. When choosing brushes for grilling, natural bristles are best, as synthetic bristles could melt. Wash these brushes with soap and water after each use. Use a sturdy scrub brush for cleaning the shells of clams and oysters. New on the market are silicone-bristled grill brushes, often paired with a vessel for holding marinades or basting sauces. The material withstands high grill

temperatures so the bristles won't be damaged from the heat.

Sieves & Strainers

Herbs must be rinsed and completely dried before chopping; a salad spinner does a very good job. The most common use for a colander is to drain foods cooked in water. In grilling it plays many roles, from holding salted eggplant while the bitter juices drain away to supporting a duck while it is doused with boiling water to remove excess fat. Use a fine-mesh wire sieve to drain finely cut foods and to strain stocks and sauces.

Miscellaneous Equipment

These specialized tools accomplish specific tasks. Fish tweezers are used to pull out thin bones from fish fillets. A funnel makes quick work of transferring

liquids, such as the barbecue sauce on page 93, to serving bottles.

Every kitchen needs a medium-sized pair of tongs, just right for turning food in a frying pan. Long tongs will help you reach into tall stockpots to move ingredients as needed, but they can also be very helpful on the grill, where shorter tongs could be hard to manage in the intense heat.

A rasp grater, such as a Microplane grater, is essential for grating the zest of citrus into fine shreds. A wooden citrus reamer helps to quickly remove the juice from lemons, limes, and oranges.

Two thermometers (not pictured) are good for testing the doneness of meats and poultry: a digital probe thermometer, which can remain in the food as it cooks, and a less-costly instant-read thermometer, which cannot.

Glossary

AIOLI A pungent garlic-flavored mayonnaise popular in the south of France.

ALMONDS Found inside the pit of a dry fruit related to peaches, almonds have a pointed, oval shape and a delicate fragrance. They are available whole, sliced (flaked), blanched (with skins removed) and slivered.

AVOCADO Rich in flavor and texture, avocados are most commonly available in two varieties: California's dark green, dimpled Hass avocado and the smoother, paler green Fuerte. Hass avocados boast the highest oil content and will produce the best results in guacamole (page 51).

BABY BACK RIBS Pork ribs taken from the center section of the loin. They are smaller, less meaty, and less fatty than spare ribs.

BEARD The little tuft of fibers a mussel uses to connect to rocks or pilings. To remove it, cut and scrape it with a knife or scissors.

BOUQUET GARNI A French term referring to a bundle of herbs and/or spices added to a stock or sauce to perfume it with flavor.

BUTTERFLYING The technique of cutting food nearly all the way through so that, instead of being split into two pieces, it will lie relatively flat.

BUTTER, UNSALTED Butter that is unsalted is preferable to salted as it allows you more control in seasoning a dish. In addition, the unsalted butter tends to be fresher, as the salt acts as a preservative, lengthening the shelf life of butter at the supermarket. Refrigerate unsalted butter in its original wrapping for up to 6 weeks.

BRINE Water that has been heavily salted and then flavored with herbs, spices, or sugar depending on its purpose. The term "brining" means to immerse food in a brine to preserve or flavor it.

BROTH & STOCK Commercially produced, well-flavored liquids made by cooking meat, poultry, fish, or vegetables in water. Canned broths tend to be saltier than homemade, so seek out a high-quality brand that offers a

"low-sodium" or "reduced-sodium" product for better control of the seasoning in your dish. You can also purchase excellent "homemade" stocks in fresh or frozen quantities from upscale supermarkets and specialty-food stores.

CAPERS Capers are the unopened flower buds of bushes native to the Mediterranean. The buds are dried, cured, and then usually packed in a vinegar brine. Capers are also sold packed in salt; rinse them thoroughly before using. Nonpareil capers, especially small capers from southern France, are considered by many cooks to be the finest.

CAYENNE A very hot ground red pepper made from dried cayenne and other chiles, cayenne is used sparingly to add heat or to heighten flavor. Always begin with a small amount and add more to taste in small increments.

CHEESES A good cheese shop is a rewarding experience, since you'll be able to taste a variety of types before you buy. Store cheeses in a warmer part of the refrigerator, like the door, wrapped in parchment (baking) or waxed paper rather than plastic, to allow them to breathe.

Blue Cheese that is inoculated with spores of special molds to develop a fine network of blue veins for a strong, sharp, peppery flavor and a crumbly texture.

Cheddar First made in Cheddar, England, this cheese is appreciated for its tangy, salty flavor, which ranges from mild to extra-sharp, depending on age. Although naturally a creamy white color, Cheddar is often died orange.

Feta A young cheese traditionally made from sheep's milk and known for its crumbly texture. Feta's saltiness is heightened by the brine in which the cheese is packed.

Parmigiano-Reggiano This firm, aged, salty cheese is made from partially skimmed cow's milk. It has a rich, nutty flavor and a pleasant, granular texture and is the most renowned of all Parmesan cheeses.

CHILE POWDER A pure powder made by grinding a single specific variety of dried chile. Ancho and New Mexico chile powders are the most common. Seek out chipotle chile powder for a particularly smoky flavor. Do not confuse chile powder with chili powder, typically a blend of powdered dried chile, oregano, cumin, and other seasonings.

CHILES Fresh chiles range in size from tiny to large, and in heat intensity from mild to fiery hot. Select firm, bright-colored chiles with blemish-free skins. To reduce the heat of a chile, remove the ribs and seeds, where the heat-producing compound, called capsaicin, resides. When working with hot chiles, wear a latex glove to avoid burning your skin, then wash your hands and any utensils thoroughly with hot, soapy water the moment you finish.

Chipotle A dried and smoked jalapeño chile, with lots of flavor and lots of heat. These dark brown chiles are about 3 inches (7.5 cm) long and are sold either dried whole or ground, packed in an oniony tomato mixture called adobo sauce.

Jalapeño This fresh hot chile measures 2–4 inches (5–10 cm) long, has a generous amount of flesh, and ranges from mildly hot to fiery. Green jalapeños are widely available in supermarkets.

Scotch bonnet Smaller than the habanero, only 1–1½ (2.5–4cm) inches in length, the Scotch bonnet is extremely hot. The little round fresh chiles are green, yellow, orange, or red. Use Scotch bonnets interchangeably with habeneros or 3 or 4 jalapenos.

CHILI SAUCE Not to be confused with Asian chile sauces, this American-style sauce is a mild ketchuplike blend of tomatoes, chili powder, onions, green bell peppers (capsicums), vinegar, sugar, and spices. Look for chili sauce near the condiments in the supermarket.

CHORIZO Coarsley ground spicy pork sausage used in Mexican and Spanish cooking. It's best to remove the casings before cooking.

CLAMS, LITTLENECK There are two varieties available on the market. The smallest of the hard-shelled clam family, Atlantic littlenecks measure 1½–1¼ inches (4–6 cm) in diameter. These are particularly sweet and are eaten raw or very gently cooked. Pacific littlenecks that are harvested from Mexico to Alaska are also known as Pacific clams and are about the same size.

COLESLAW A salad of finely shredded cabbage mixed with mayonnaise dressing.

CORNSTARCH This is a highly refined, silky powder, also known as cornflour, made from corn kernels and is most commonly used to thicken sauces. It has nearly twice the thickening power of flour and gives sauces a glossy sheen, unlike the opaque finish of a flour-thickened sauce.

COUNTRY-STYLE RIBS Large, meaty pork ribs cut from the rib end or sirloin and sold as individual ribs or slabs.

CURRY POWDER Typical ingredients in this ground spice blend from South Asia include turmeric, cumin, coriander, pepper, cardamom, mustard, cloves, and ginger. Curry powders are categorized as mild, hot, and very hot. Madras curry powder is a well-balanced version with medium heat.

EGGPLANT The most familiar globe eggplant (aubergine) is usually large, egg or pear shaped, with a skin that looks almost black.

FISH SAUCE A clear liquid used in southeast Asian cooking and as a table condiment, much like soy sauce. It ranges in color from amber to dark brown and has a pungent aroma and strong salty flavor.

GARLIC When buying garlic, choose plump, firm heads with no brown discoloration. (A tinge of purple is fine, even desirable.) Always take care not to cook garlic beyond a light gold, or it can taste harsh and bitter.

GINGER A refreshing combination of spicy and sweet in both aroma and flavor, ginger adds a lively note to many recipes, particularly Asian dishes. Select ginger that is firm and heavy and has a smooth skin.

HERBS Using fresh herbs is one of the best things you can do to improve your cooking. Dried herbs do have their place, but fresh herbs usually bring brighter flavors to a dish.

Basil Used in kitchens throughout the Mediterranean and in Southeast Asia, fresh basil adds a highly aromatic, peppery flavor.

Chives These slender, hollow, grasslike blades are used to give an onionlike flavor to dishes, without the bite.

Cilantro Also called fresh coriander or Chinese parsley, cilantro has a bright astringent taste. It is used extensively in Mexican, Asian, Indian, Latin, and Middle Eastern cuisines.

Dill This herb has fine, feathery leaves with a distinct aromatic flavor.

Fresh vs. dried Use fresh herbs to season pastes, sauces, and marinades. Dried herbs are best in spice rubs, especially if you intend to store them. When substituting fresh for dried herbs, double the amount.

Herbes de Provence A dried herb blend popular in southern France. The mixture can contain a combination of any of the following: basil, fennel seed, lavender, marjoram, rosemary, sage, summer savory, and thyme.

Lemongrass An aromatic herb used in much of Southeast Asia, it resembles a green (spring) onion in shape but has a fresh lemony aroma and flavor. Use only the pale green bottom part for cooking. Since fibers are tough, lemongrass needs to be removed much like a bay leaf.

Mint This refreshing herb is available in many varieties, with spearmint the most commonly found.

Oregano Aromatic and spicy herb also known as wild marjoram. It is one of the few herbs that keeps its flavor when dried.

Parsley, flat-leaf Also known as Italian parsley, this dark green Italian variety of the faintly peppery herb adds vibrant color and pleasing flavor to many hors d'oeuvres.

Rosemary This woody Mediterranean herb, with leaves like pine needles, has an assertive flavor. Always use in moderation.

Sage The soft, gray-green leaves of this Mediterranean herb are sweet and aromatic.

Tarragon The slender, delicate, deep green leaves of tarragon impart an elegant, aniselike scent.

Thyme Tiny green leaves on thin stems, this herb is a mild, all-purpose seasoning. Its floral, earthy flavor complements meats, fish, vegetables. If a large amount is needed, gently pull the leaves backward off the stem with one motion. When the thyme stems are young and still very soft, you can chop them along with the leaves, but more mature stems will be woody.

HOISIN SAUCE This spicy, slightly sweet, brownish red sauce is made from fermented soybeans enlivened with five-spice powder, garlic, and dried chile. It is widely available in bottles and jars in the Asian section of most supermarkets. Once opened, it will keep indefinitely in the refrigerator. Hoisin sauce is a versatile ingredient that can be used alone or added to other sauces and glazes to contribute flavor and color.

HONEY A common sweetener that varies in flavor and color, according to the flower nectar gathered by the bees. Typical light, mild honeys include clover and orange blossom, while eucalyptus and wildflower are common dark, strong honeys.

HOT-PEPPER SAUCE A splash of hot-pepper sauce adds zip to dishes. Countless varieties of hot-pepper sauce are made, with a rainbow of pepper colors and heat levels, so allow yourself the opportunity to experiment and find one you especially like.

MAHIMAHI Also known as dolphin fish or dorado, mahimahi is a blue (or green) and gold fish found in warm waters and appreciated for its excellent flavor.

MANGOES Juicy, sweet-fleshed fruit native to India and now cultivated in many other tropical regions. When shopping for ripe mangoes, choose fruits that are aromatic at their stem ends.

MAPLE SYRUP Pure maple syrup is made from the boiled sap of the sugar maple tree. The caramel-colored, maple-flavored corn syrup commonly drizzled on pancakes and waffles, often called "pancake syrup," has no relation to the real thing. Sugaring season, as it is called, usually begins in early spring and lasts at least a month or for as long as the nights are warm enough to get the sap rising. A long boiling period reduces the clear sap to a rich, aromatic, amber syrup. Good-quality maple syrup will taste like caramel and vanilla.

MARINADE A highly flavored, acid-based mixture in which meat, poultry, fish, or vegetables soak for a set amount of time to add flavor to and moisturize these foods.

MAYONNAISE A creamy cold sauce of egg yolks, oil, and lemon juice or vinegar blended into a thick emulsion.

MIRIN An important ingredient in Japanese cuisine, mirin is a sweet cooking wine made by fermenting glutinous rice and sugar. The pale gold and syrupy wine adds a rich flavor when added to a dish or dipping sauce.

MUSSELS A saltwater mollusk with slightly pointed shells ranging in color from blue green to yellowish brown to black. Mussels have cream to orange colored meat and are sweeter than oysters or clams.

MUSTARD, DIJON Originating in Dijon, France, this silky smooth and slightly tangy mustard contains brown or black mustard seeds, white wine, and herbs.

NONREACTIVE A term used to describe a pan or dish made of or lined with a material—stainless steel, enamel, ceramic, or glass—that will not react with acidic ingredients in the recipe, such as citrus juice, vinegar, wine, or tomatoes.

OIL The heat requirements and other ingredients of a recipe usually suggest which oil is appropriate to use. As a general rule, choose less-refined, more flavorful oils for uncooked uses, such as tossing raw or already cooked foods, and refined, blander oils for cooking.

Asian sesame This amber-colored oil, pressed from toasted sesame seeds, has a rich, nutty flavor. Look for it in well-stocked markets and Asian groceries.

Canola This neutral-flavored oil, notable for its monounsaturated fats, is recommended for general cooking.

Grapeseed Pressed from grape seeds and mild in flavor, this all-purpose oil heats to high temperature without smoking, making it suitable for frying, and is also used in salad dressings and marinades.

Olive Made from the first pressing of the olives without the use of heat or chemicals, extra-virgin olive oil is clear green or brownish and has a fruity, slightly peppery flavor that is used to best advantage when it will not be cooked. Olive oils extracted using heat or chemicals, then filtered and blended to eliminate much of the olives' character, may be used for general cooking. In the past, such oil was labeled "pure olive oil." Today, it is simply labeled "olive oil."

OLIVES, KALAMATA The most popular Greek variety, the Kalamata olive is almond shaped, purplish black, rich, and meaty. It is brine cured and then packed in oil or vinegar.

ONIONS This humble bulb vegetable, in the same family as leeks and garlic, is one of the most common and frequently used ingredients in the kitchen.

Green Also known as scallions or spring onions, green onions are the immature shoots of the bulb onion, with a narrow white base that has not yet begun to swell and long, flat green leaves, sometimes called "tops." They are mild in flavor.

Red These onions tend to be mild, slightly sweet, and purplish. They are delicious when used raw.

Yellow These are the familiar, all-purpose onions sold in supermarkets. Yellow onions are usually too harsh for serving raw, but they become rich and sweet when cooked.

OYSTERS These shellfish readily take on the flavor of their environments and are traditionally named after the area where they live. Buy oysters from reputable merchants who can vouch that they come from safe, unpolluted waters. Live oysters should have a mild, sweet smell; their shells should be closed and feel heavy with water.

PAPRIKA Red or orange-red, paprika is made from dried peppers. The finest paprikas come from Hungary and Spain in three basic types: sweet, medium-sweet, and hot. Sweet paprika, which is mild but still pungent, is the most versatile. The best Spanish paprika, known as *pimentón de La Vera,* is made from smoked peppers, which give it a distinctive flavor.

PARBOIL To cook food partially in boiling water, sometimes as a preparatory step before combining it with ingredients with different cooking times or finishing with another cooking method.

PECANS Native to North America, pecans have two deeply crinkled lobes of nut meat, much like the walnut. They have smooth, brown, oval shells that break easily, and their flavor is sweeter and more delicate than closely related walnuts.

PINEAPPLE Its oval shape and ridged, scalelike texture inspired the Spanish to name the pineapple after a *piña,* or pine cone. Pineapples usually weigh 3–7 pounds (1.5–3.5 kg). Look for fruits that give slightly and have deep green leaves. As pineapples ripen, they turn yellow from the bottom up.

PINE NUTS These small nuts have an elongated, slightly tapered shape and a delicate flavor. Store them in an airtight container in a cool place away from light.

PLANKING A method adopted from Native American Indians for cooking food on a board, which imparts its wood flavor to the food as it cooks. Untreated cedar and alder planks are two popular choices.

PORTOBELLO MUSHROOM Mature cremini mushrooms, portobellos have a rich smoky flavor and meat texture. The thick, tough stems should be removed before cooking.

RED BELL PEPPERS Also known as sweet peppers and capsicums, these flavorful, colorful peppers are delicious cooked on the grill. They are typically charred and then peeled, resulting in a smoky flavor. Buy firm, smooth, and bright-colored peppers.

SAKE Sometimes referred to as "Japanese rice wine" it is made from grain, not fruit, and has a relatively low alcohol count. It lends itself well to marinades and sauces.

SALMON A meaty, oily, firm fish that is best from the wild. Farm-raised salmon is weaned on additives and color enhancers and lacks good flavor.

SALT Table salt is usually amended with iodine and with additives that enable it to flow freely. While many cooks prefer kosher or sea salt for seasoning, table salt works well in brines because the size of the grains are consistent and easily dissolved.

Fleur de sel One of the most prized sea salts, it is from Brittany. It has a grayish ivory color and has more flavor than kosher or regular sea salt.

Kosher With a superior flavor to table salt, kosher salt has large flakes that are easy to grasp. Since it is not as salty, kosher salt can be used more liberally than table salt.

Sea Available in coarse or fine grains, this salt is produced naturally by evaporation. It dissolves more readily than kosher salt.

SATAY Popular in Southeast Asia, satay are strips of meat or poultry threaded onto skewers, grilled, and served with a spicy peanut-based dipping sauce.

SAUVIGNON BLANC Crisp white wine high in acid with herbaceous or grassy overtones. Goes well with fish and shellfish and also in sauces.

SHALLOTS These small members of the onion family look like large cloves of garlic covered with papery bronze or reddish skin. Shallots have white flesh streaked with purple, a crisp texture, and a flavor more subtle than that of onions.

SHRIMP Although often sold peeled and deveined, it's best to purchase shrimp (prawns) still in their shells if possible. Most shrimp have been previously frozen, and the shells help preserve their texture and flavor.

SIMMER When liquid is maintained at a temperature just below boil. Tiny bubbles breaking on the surface indicate the liquid has reached a simmer.

SPARERIBS A fatty pork cut from the lower portion of the rib cage. Spareribs are best when grilled over a slow, smoky fire.

SPICES An important part of any spice pantry, seeds, used whole or ground, add flavor, aroma, and texture to marinades, rubs, and other preparations.

Aniseed The seed of the anise plant, a member of the parsley family, aniseed has a licorice taste.

Coriander The dried ripe fruit of fresh coriander, or cilantro, these tiny, round, ridged seeds have an exotic flavor.

Cumin The seed of a member of the parsley family, cumin adds a sharp flavor to many Latin American and Indian dishes.

Fennel This mediterranean spice has a sweet aniselike flavor and is used to enhance the flavors in meat, chicken, and fish.

Five spice Sometimes labeled "Chinese five-spice powder," this potent spice blend varies in its makeup but usually contains cloves, aniseeds or fennel seeds, star anise, cinnamon, Sichuan peppercorns, and sometimes ginger.

Garlic powder Ground, dried garlic cloves used to season meat and fish.

Onion powder Ground dried onion used as a seasoning in spice rubs.

Star anise A dried star-shaped seedpod of a Chinese evergreen tree related to the magnolia. It is slightly more bitter than aniseed and has a distinct licorice flavor that pairs well with meats.

SWORDFISH Large, firm, mild-flavored fish with a meatlike texture.

TERIYAKI A bottled sweet sauce that is used as a glaze or sauce to accompany nearly any grilled food. You can easily make a home version by mixing equal parts sake, mirin (sweet cooking wine), or sherry and dark soy sauce with sugar to taste.

TROUT Delicate, somewhat oily freshwater fish that can be cooked whole on a grill.

TUNA There are four types of tuna sold commercially and each is unique in its own way. Albacore, a white-fleshed tuna; yellowfin, also referred to as ahi, from the Hawaiian Islands; bluefin, usually the most expensive because it is the highest in fat; and bigeye, the most versatile tuna on the market, and similar to the bluefin.

VINEGAR Many types of vinegar are available, made from a variety of wines or, like rice vinegar, from grains. They often add just the right amount of tartness to a dish.

Balsamic This aged vinegar is made from the unfermented grape juice of white Trebbiano grapes. Balsamic is aged for as little as 1 year or for as long as 75 years; the vinegar slowly evaporates and grows sweeter and mellower.

White Wine A pantry staple carried in most supermarkets, white wine vinegar is created by allowing white wine to ferment naturally over a period of months

WORCESTERSHIRE SAUCE A traditional English condiment, Worcestershire sauce is an intensely flavored, savory blend of varied ingredients, including molasses, soy sauce, garlic, onion, and anchovies.

ZEST The colored portion of citrus peel that is rich in flavorful oils. The white portion of the peel, called the pith, is bitter. When choosing citrus for zesting, look for organic fruits, since pesticides concentrate in thin skins.

Index

FREE PRESS

A Division of Simon & Schuster, Inc.
1230 Avenue of the Americas
New York, NY 10020

WILLIAMS-SONOMA

Founder & Vice-Chairman Chuck Williams

WELDON OWEN INC.

Chief Executive Officer John Owen
President and Chief Operating Officer Terry Newell
Chief Financial Officer Christine E. Munson
Vice President International Sales Stuart Laurence
Creative Director Gaye Allen
Publisher Hannah Rahill
Senior Editor Jennifer Newens
Associate Editor Lauren Higgins
Art Director Kyrie Forbes
Designers Adrienne Aquino and Andrea Stephany
Production Director Chris Hemesath
Color Manager Teri Bell
Production and Reprint Coordinator Todd Rechner
Food Stylist Kevin Crafts
Prop Stylist Leigh Nöe
Assistant Food Stylist Luis Bustamante
Assistant Food Stylist and Hand Model Katie Christ

PHOTO CREDITS

Tucker & Hossler, all photography, except the following:
Mark Thomas: page 32, 36 (citrus sequence),
37, 41 (crosshatching sequence), 42 (visual doneness
sequence), 135 (top and bottom left).
Bill Bettencourt: page 33, 35, 36
(nuts and seeds sequence), 135 (top right).

THE MASTERING SERIES

Conceived and produced by Weldon Owen Inc.
814 Montgomery Street, San Francisco, CA 94133
Telephone: 415 291 0100 Fax: 415 291 8841

In collaboration with Williams-Sonoma, Inc.
3250 Van Ness Avenue, San Francisco, CA 94109

A WELDON OWEN PRODUCTION
Copyright © 2006 by Weldon Owen Inc. and Williams-Sonoma Inc.

All rights reserved, including the right of reproduction in whole or in part
in any form.

FREE PRESS and colophon are registered trademarks of Simon & Schuster, Inc.

For information regarding special discounts for bulk purchases,
please contact Simon & Schuster Special Sales at 1 800 456 6798 or
business@simonandschuster.com

Set in ITC Berkeley and FF The Sans.

Color separations by Embassy Graphics.
Printed and bound in China by SNP Leefung Printers Limited.

First printed in 2006.

10 9 8 7 6 5 4 3 2 1

Library of Congress Cataloging-in-Publication data is available.

ISBN–13: 978-0-7432-7107-3
ISBN–10: 0-7432-7107-6

ACKNOWLEDGMENTS

Weldon Owen wishes to thank the following people for their
generous support in producing this book: Desne Ahlers,
Ken DellaPenta, Leslie Evans, Lesli Nielson, Stephanie Rosenbaum,
and Sharon Silva.

A NOTE ON WEIGHTS AND MEASURES

All recipes include customary U.S. and metric measurements. Metric conversions are based on
a standard developed for these books and have been rounded off. Actual weights may vary.